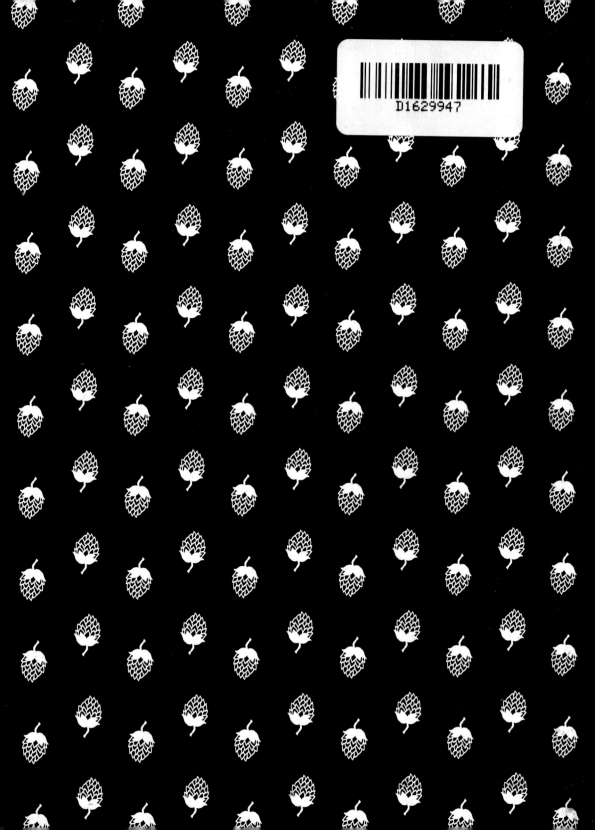

MIKKEL BORG BJERGSØ AND PERNILLE PANG

Mikkeller's
BOOK OF
BEER

PHOTOGRAPHY
Rasmus Malmstrøm and Camilla Stephan

ILLUSTRATOR
Keith Shore

jacqui
small

Twenty years ago, a lot of beer (most often lager) tasted the same across the world. Whether Tuborg, Tsingtao, Budweiser or Heineken, it was pale in colour, weak in flavour and low in alcohol, and for the most part consumed either to quench thirst or to get drunk. Today, the situation is very different. Courtesy of the craft microbrewing revolution that spread during the 1990s from the US and the UK to the rest of Europe, particularly the Nordic countries, and then to the rest of the world, the beer scene now is home to a diverse band of brewers and beer enthusiasts who live and breathe the hopped beverage. One of the figureheads of this revolution is Mikkel Borg Bjergsø, the man behind the Mikkeller microbrewery that, since 2006, has helped change the general perception of beer to the point where it now takes in not only weaker-tasting lagers, but also highly-hopped India Pale Ales and bone-dry lambics.

Mikkeller's Book of Beer has been written with the indispensable assistance of numerous experts from Mikkeller's colourful team, but essentially it is the product of a close collaboration between Mikkel and me. I met Mikkel before he had caught a whiff of the hop. Today, we are married with two daughters, and it was at home in our apartment in Vesterbro, Copenhagen, that it all started back in 2003. That was the year in which Mikkel and his childhood friend Kristian Klarup Keller began experimenting with home brewing in our kitchen, where I occasionally helped to bottle, cap and label the beer. Subsequently, I trained as a journalist, and, as Mikkeller grew, it became more and more obvious that I should tell the fascinating story of the maths and physics teacher who became world-famous as a nomadic brewer and a craft beer evangelist. His 'democratic principles' of brewing allow anyone to brew their own beer at home, at relatively little cost.

In the following pages, you can read Mikkel's story of how he found his way into the world of beer, how Mikkeller started and subsequently developed into one of the world's leading microbreweries. Above all, though, you can read about beer, because this is first and foremost an inspiring guidebook for anyone who is interested in beer in any way, whether those who aspire to learn more about this versatile beverage or those who dream of brewing exciting, great-tasting beer at home.

PERNILLE PANG
February 2014

Mikkel Borg Bjergsø

CHAPTER 1

FROM 'BUCKET BOY' TO STELLAR BREWER
THE STORY OF MIKKEL AND MIKKELLER

For as long as I can remember, I've had a competitive gene. If I can see that I'm good at something, I'm always trying to get better. I can't help myself. I've always preferred the type of sport that is measurable. Which is why I think I started running. Football is so much about chance and teamwork. In running, who's best is not open to debate. It's always the person who comes first.

My twin brother, Jeppe, and I were close companions all through our childhood and part of our adolescence. Our parents divorced when we were eight, and we stayed in a single-family detached house with my mother, while my father moved to North Jutland, remarried and had two more children. Jeppe and I started in the same preschool class at Nivå Centralskole, but the teachers quickly agreed that it was best to split us up. By all accounts, we were too domineering. We were twice as 'big', 'strong' and 'loud' as all the other children. And although we regularly fell out, we always backed one another up against the other children. If anyone said anything bad about Jeppe, I was always on his side, and vice versa. But we also competed with one another. Initially, it was mostly for fun, like when we timed each other when we had to empty the dishwasher at home.

When as teenagers we both began to do athletics, the competition became more serious. I remember one time at the Aarhus Games when the judges ruled that I had beaten Jeppe by one hundredth of a second. You couldn't tell from the photo-finish image, so we shouted and screamed at one another. We were always being compared, so it wasn't much fun when one of us wasn't quite as good as the other.

A RUNNER'S WORLD

For about 10 years – from 1987 to 1997 – we spent most weekends training and attending meetings, and we both became multiple

Danish champions. As 14-year-olds, we attended a meeting where we met Kristian Keller (known as Keller) and Brian Jensen, who ran for the Viking Club in Bornholm. We quickly became friends, and Jeppe and I started spending holidays with them in Bornholm.

When I began at Espergærde Gymnasium upper-secondary school, I got up every morning at five o'clock, put on my training kit and was out of the door in just five minutes. I then ran 10 kilometres (6 miles) on the asphalt path alongside the train line and fields from Nivå to Kokkedal. I did that every single day, even if it was hammering down or there was snow and frost on the ground. After the run, I took a quick bath and wolfed down a bowl of oatmeal with milk and sugar before catching the train to Espergærde. Three or four evenings a week, I trained at the Sparta sports club in Østerbro, otherwise I went to my girlfriend's house in Vanløse. If I had homework, I often did it on the train there and back. When I had PE at school, I was allowed to do running instead. In total, I trained 12 times a week; twice a day on weekdays and once on Saturday and Sunday respectively. I ran middle-distance events – 800 metres and 1500 metres – and my aim was always to beat my competitors, including Jeppe.

When Jeppe and I became students, we both went to the USA after winning running scholarships to American universities. Keller and Brian also won scholarships for the USA, so we continued to see a lot of one another both at athletics meetings and in our leisure time, even though our universities were in different parts of the country. I spent several hours a day in the long, narrow corridor of my dormitory talking on the phone with Keller.

After a year in Kansas, I returned home to Denmark. I was tired and injured, and I thought the university was too demanding. Jeppe also returned home, and we moved into an apartment together in

BUNDEN I VEJRET

Skål for Mikkeller - verdens sjette bedste bryggeri, startet af Mikkel Bjergso, der også laver Danmarks stærkeste øl. FOTO: HENNING HJORTH.

Øl med mange procenter

Mikro-bryggeriet Mikkeller har sendt Danmarks stærkeste øl på gaden

Kristian Korn[o]

Når Danmarks stærkeste øl løber forbi ganen, bliver smagsløgene bombarderet med en mørk sødme med en snert af kaffebønner og chokolade. 'Het' hedder dråberne med en alkoholprocent på 17,5, og de er brygget af Mikkeller. Mikrobryggeriets har lavet 'Het', som betyder sort på kinesisk, for at lave en øl, der rykker grænser.

Smagsmæssigt er ølen slidsyg, men meget vellykket. Det er en øl på alles præmisser og ikke lavet til det brede publikum, fortæller Mikkel Bjergso.

Øl-oprør

Til daglig arbejder den unge øl-brygger som lærer på Det Frie Gymnasium i København, men en aften i maj 20[..] kastede han og kammeraten, Kristian Keller, sig ud i bryggekunsten. De ville gøre op med mikrobryggeriernes Carlsberg-agtige me[...]

de det, siger han.

Siden er springet fra hobby-bryggere til øl-stjerner gået stærkt. En dag opfordrede indehaveren af Ølbutikken i Oehlenschlægersgade venner ne til at hælde deres bryg på flaske. Ølhermo blev revet væk, og siden har de lejet sig ind på mikrobryggerier for at lave øl i større mængder.

Verdens sjettebedste

Selv om ølen stadig bliver udviklet hjemme i køkkenet på Vesterbro, så er Mikkeller lige blevet kåret til verdens sjettebedste bryggeri foran 8000 andre på den internationale øl-hjemmeside, Ratebeer.com.

Den gode placering på Ratebeer.com har gjort, at ølen i dag bliver eksporteret til 11 forskellige lande.

— Succesen har været overvældende, og jeg overvejer også at blive brygger på fuld tid. Jeg var bare slet ikke beredt på meningen, da vi lavede de første øl hjemme i køkkenet, fortæller Mikkel Bjergso.

Bryggeren hviler heller ikke på humlen, for han har allerede planer om at forsøge sig med en øl på omkring 20 procent. Grænserne skal hele tiden rykkes, så ølentusiaster over hele verden kan få udfordret deres smagsløg. Skål.

WILDC[...]

Mikkel Bjergso races through the course at Warner Park. Bjergso finished in 36th place, while rac[...] ever Big Eight Championships. Overall, the men's team finished in 7th place. Geoff Delahanty capt[...]

[...]s 3rd [...]ffort

[...]us if it wasn't for [...]well," Drake said.

[...]with the overall [...]English and Norwegian [...]d a medal.

[...]ything that was that [...]ing in the top 10,"

[...]was almost there, [...] runners with a time

[...]rmance was just

[...] hope I do better at

[...]he finish line of [...]e teammates Irma [...]ene Ragan in 17th. [...] happy with her [...]ecially pleased with

[...]

runner, senior Billy Waggaaer, experienced side cramps, which caused him to run a sub-par race.

"Billy ran really bad because he stitched up," Drake said.

"If he would have been where he's capable of placing, we would have accomplished our goal of placing well."

The ailing Waggaaer finished in 38th position behind teammates junior Geoff Delahanty in 30th and freshman Mikkel Bjergso in 36th.

Delahanty said although he was the highest finisher for the Cats, he was still not altogether pleased with his showing.

"People have been telling me that I ran a good race," Delahanty said. "It was probably the best finish in a race that I've had, but it's still not even close to as good as I can run.

"I might have gotten a little overzealous and just ran a little too quick sometimes."

Delahanty said if Waggaaer and himself had run to their potential, the outcome of the race would have been much different.

"Billy could have been top 10 easy, and I could have been top 15, if we would have run like we've been in practice," Waggaaer said.

Iowa State dominated the meet with o[...] giving them the championship.

Waggaaer said the overall place of the [...] matter as much as giving the younger [...] experience.

"Since we have a lot of freshmen and so [...] now, it's not really that important righ n [...] said. "As long as they get to know how the [...] and observe, then they'll be fine."

Entering the NCAA District V Champi [...] said he has a completely different outlook [...]

Drake said he is hoping to take the wom [...] NCAA Championships.

"For the next two weeks, we'll focu[...] We'll lower the mileage some and maybe [...] a little," Drake said.

In the men's division, Drake said he is [...] about the team's chances.

"What we're really going to focus on [...] nationals and have Jeff and Mikkel run [...] said. "We're going to take a weekend to tr[...]

[...] and field and cross country honors in both track [...] [...] during his career as a [...] Olive-Smith, a native of South Africa qualified for the NCAA Cross Country Championship[...] last season and consistently challenged O'Neill for the top spot on [...]

[...] "The first couple of years I didn't really start [...] [...] training hard until August," Wagg[...] [...] year I never slowed down."

The brothers have trained together since they were children, but Bjergso said their really isn't any competition between the two of them.

"We don't beat me in a race since we were young, but it doesn't really beat me," I glad it's him and not someone else," Bjergso said. "We like [...]

Bjergso competed in several track club centered in Copenhagen, the capital of Denmark.

He said he joined the club after previously running for the club after hometown of Nivaa because the chance to compete is better there.

"There are no school teams in Denmark," Bjergso said. "You have to run in a club.

"The club in Nivaa was too small and didn't offer much."

The transition to the new culture has

like to go to the same school together, but after awhile we were together all the time and we got sick of each other."

Opportunity is the bigger reason Bjergso wanted to come to the United States to compete.

He said American track meets offer better competition.

"The competition here is so much better in Denmark," Bjergso said. "Some of the times that I thought were pretty fast in Denmark aren't anything special here."

Bjergso started his quest to compete in America by writing out letters with his autobiography to several colleges around the nation.

Coach Drake received one of the letters and phoned Bjergso in Denmark.

After speaking with several other coaches, Bjergso said he knew that he wanted to compete for Drake.

"After I told other State, they wanted to say [...] the school. It seemed kind [...] nab."

[...] been smooth.

[...] He is fluent in [...] English and [...] and Norwegian.

[...] "America [...] the Danish,"

[...] The people [...] way to" be [...] boryan in De [...] The transit [...] of education [...] somewhat [...]

[...] "I have [...] English, but [...] difficult.

[...] "I will [...] in a different [...] major [...]

As far as [...] Bjergso said [...] earning a de [...] engineering [...] interest in m[...]

Mikkel Bjergso trains for the cross country season. The season opens Sept. 17 at Lincoln, Neb.

PHILLY CAMPBELL/Collegian

K-State's cross country coach finds the runner he needs in

Runner recruited by coach over the phone by mail

WESS NIGELSON
Collegian

With one new runner returning to the men's cross country team, Coach Terry Drake needed help.

Drake found the help he needed, but it wasn't about one expensive way distance or one call.

Mikkel Bjergso, freshman from Nivaa, Denmark, has found his way to Manhattan, where he began to continue an already successful running career.

In Denmark, Bjergso captured nine national junior championships in cross country and track.

However, to attend K-State, Bjergso had to separate from his twin brother, Jeppe, who earned a cross country and track scholarship at Arkansas State, Ark.

"Last spring, we thought we would

DENMA[RK]

THE BEER NUT

2 – Oktober 2003   Officiel BØF avis   Sælges ikke i løssalg

Løsslupne svinehunde side 6-7

Når øllet gærer i stuen side 4-5

Sveriges hemmelighed side 8-9

Ølanmeldelser side 10-11

... og meget mere

Mikkeller

Mikkels sorte guld

32-årig har udskiftet mesterskaberne på løbebanen med øl-priser

Morten Mauritson

Det er lidt billigt at stjæle W.C. Fields-citatet "Øllet blev hans skæbne", men det passer bare så uendelig godt på et af landets største løbetalenter, der blev skolelærer og Mikkeller-bryggeriet.

I halvfemserne gjorde han sig bemærket på landets atletik-stadioner som en af landets bedste mellemdistanceløbere, men den karriere blev udskiftet med skolelærerfaget.

Som så mange andre er han vild med øl, og det resulterede i, at ølklubben med vennerne blev til eget bryg i køkkenet og nu store produktioner i eksempelvis Ørbæk, Belgien og Norge. Det er også blevet til et gæstebryg på Nørrebro Bryghus.

produktioner i eksempelvis Ørbæk, Belgien og Norge. Det er også blevet til et gæstebryg på Nørrebro Bryghus.

Provokerende øl

32-årige Mikkel Bjergsø er navnet på manden, der i dag er anerkendt for sit bryg i store dele af verden.

Man behøver ikke være ølentusiast for at drikke Mikkels øl, men det hjælper, for han er mest til kompromisløse og provokerende øl.

– Der skal sgu være noget kant, og det skal ikke blive for fint. Masser af bryggerier laver helt almindeligt øl, så det gider jeg ikke. Man kan godt sige, at jeg overdriver lidt, når jeg brygger, men det

en, men i dag er vi også mange flere bryggere rundt omkring, fordi det er muligt at producere sit eget bryg hjemme i køkkenet. Det vælter frem med mikrobryggerier, og mange af os har det som en slags hobby-beskæftigelse, selv om det for mig mere er et fuldtidsjob i brygger.

– Nej, jeg ligner ikke den klassiske brygger fra tv-serien.

motor2@bf.dk

er også det, der har gjort, at der er blevet lagt mærke til mit bryg ude i verden, og det er jeg meget stolt af, fortæller Mikkel Bjergsø, der henslænger i caféstolen på Nørrebro Bryghus bestemt ligner en skolelærer – og langtfra en brygger.

Jeg er sgu min egen

Mikkel Bjergsø brygger gerne på store anlæg på bryggerier som Ørbæk på Fyn eller i udlandet, men han vil altid have sit helt eget kæmpebryggeri.

– Jeg kan godt lide den uafhængighed og frihed, jeg har nu. Jeg skal ikke tænke en kæmpe økonomi, men kan koncentrere mig om at brygge, når jeg har lejet mig

Mikkel, der ikke længere har tid til at holde konditallet oppe med løbetræning.

– Jeg passer jo mit fuldtidsjob på Det frie Gymnasium på Nørrebro, hvor jeg netop nu underviser i 8. klasse. Det er et job, jeg er helt vild med. Men jeg er så helt vild med at brygge, så det er mit andet fuldtidsjob lige nu.

Nybrygger og skolelærer

Der er stor interesse for mit bryg, så jeg bruger meget tid på at producere og distribuere til hele verden, siger den unge brygger, der gerne ser, du nipper en etiket, når du skal have en fyrraftenshøjer.

moma

Bryg i topklasse

1. Mikkel Bjergsø vandt i midten af 1990'erne flere danmarksmesterskaber i mellemdistanceløb, fortrinsvis på 1500 meter.

2. Sammen med kammeraten Kristian Keller startede hobbybryggeren eget bryggeri for et par år siden og fik øjeblikkelig megasucces.

3. Bryghuset Mikkeller blev kåret til Danmarks bedste bryghus i 2008.

4. Mikkeller er netop blevet kåret til verdens 6. bedste hjemmeside på ratebeer.com, der giver hans bryg meget fine anmeldelser.

5. Læs mere om Mikkel Bjergsø og hans stærke øl i kup! på lørdag.

Den unge brygger foran en af de store 1000-liters tanke på Nørrebro Bryghus, hvor et gæstebryg med hans signatur står og hygger sig. FOTO: MORTEN MAURITSON

PERBRYGGER OG SKOLELÆRER

Ny humle Mikkel Bjergsø i hjemmet med sin søn og Danmarks stærkeste øl. Den hedder Hei, der betyder sort på kinesisk. Og sort er øllet, hvis alkoholprocent er hele 17,5 procent. FOTO: HENNING HJORTH

Århusgade in the Østerbro district of Copenhagen and both got jobs in the canteen at Bispebjerg Hospital. Every morning at six o'clock, I ran to the hospital, where I made mashed potatoes and øllebrød, a dish made of rye bread, sugar and non-alcoholic beer, in 200-litre (53-gallon) pots and baked 1200 rolls every day. I finished work at two o'clock in the afternoon, then ran all the way home, via Bispebjerg and around Hellerup, to Østerbro. I did that for six months until I ended up on dish washing, where it was really damp and steamy. I began having breathing problems, my doctor diagnosed exercise-induced asthma and I was off sick for three months.

At that time, I was really fed up with Copenhagen. Everyone I spent time with was always talking about running and I wanted to meet new people. I also had a girlfriend who lived in North Jutland, so I decided to move there and started teacher training at Aalborg Seminarium. The course looked fairly easy to get through without a lot of effort, which suited me perfectly because I'd had enough of self-discipline after so much running. I needed the freedom to do things other than reading and writing assignments.

I did carry on doing a bit of running, but I didn't feel particularly motivated and my asthma was bothering me. All the same, I decided to up sticks again when I was offered a new scholarship by Mobile University in Alabama. The only problem was that the air humidity there was ridiculously high, which meant I couldn't breathe properly at all when I ran. I didn't get an awful lot of training and gave a poor account of myself. I also neglected my studies and just slept all day until it was time to run. Apart from that, I partied with the other students. One day, I even caught myself sleeping against a wall during a written exam. That's when I decided to go home again. I went running for the last time on 11 December 1997.

BJØRNEBRYG

Back in Copenhagen, I moved into a one-room apartment in Slesvigs-gade in Vesterbro and continued my teacher training at Frederiksberg

Seminarium. Jeppe already had an apartment with the same housing association, and a number of my friends from the Seminarium also moved in (although Keller and Brian had stayed in the USA). I was completely broke, so I started working instead of attending lessons at the Seminarium. At one point, I had three jobs on the go at the same time. I was also partying a lot, and friends from the Seminarium visited on Thursdays, Fridays and Saturdays. That's how I met Pernille, whom I later married and with whom I had two daughters; she knew someone from the Seminarium who invited her round to my place.

Every so often, my friends and I took the ten-kroner bus trip to Germany, where you could buy a box of beer really cheaply. We would buy 30 or 40 boxes at a time. We paid in the kiosk on the ferry and had the beer delivered down on the deck, where we loaded it straight into the bus. The fridge at home was always packed with beer. It just had to be as cheap as possible. As well as cans, we drank Bjørnebryg (Bear Beer), which at the time we thought tasted pretty good.

Jeppe and I also began hanging out at Café Oonas in Enghave Plads. One of their special offers was a bucket of ten foreign beers for DKK 150 (£16/US$26). They were Belgian and German beers such as Chimay, Hoegaarden and Erdinger, which tasted different to the beers we normally drank. At Oonas, we were called the 'bucket boys' because we always ordered a bucket. We generally went there every Friday and Saturday before going on into town for a concert at Vega or a party at the Seminarium. I ended up getting a job as a waiter at the café. As I was there all the time anyway, I thought I might as well work there, even though I'm sure I never really got paid any wages because I always managed to drink them away first.

BREW THE BEER

A few years later, Jeppe had the idea of starting a beer society. It was named the 'Brew the Beer Society', known by the Danish acronym BØF. The name was an in-joke at the expense of one of the club's members, a South African called Myles who spoke really good Danish

but liked to fool around with the word order. We met up five or six times a year, often in a function room in my building. It was a run-down, dark basement room, around 20 square metres (23 square yards) in area, with a small kitchen at one end and a smashed-up concrete floor. We called it 'The Hole'.

For the most part, BØF was obviously about 'stuffing ourselves silly' and 'necking beers', but it was a bit more than that. We arranged a number of blind tastings of beers in various categories such as 'best Danish beer' and 'best Christmas beer'. We would each take along a beer wrapped in silver foil, then taste the beers and award them points. After seven years in the USA and a year in Portugal, Keller had at last come home to Denmark and moved into the same building. He had studied journalism in the USA, and it was he who had the idea of producing the members magazine Beer Nut, which contained beer reviews, cartoons and reports on our visits to various microbreweries.

THE PHYSICS EXPERIMENTERS

In 2002, when I was 26, I graduated from Frederiksberg Seminarium as a schoolteacher. The following year, I got a job at Det frie Gymnasium (The Free Upper Secondary School) in Nørrebro teaching maths, physics and English. Close to the school, in Nørrebrogade, a new beer bar had opened, Plan B, which had an exciting selection of beers. Sometimes, I would drop in after work for a beer, and one day I tried an India Pale Ale (IPA) from the Danish microbrewery Brøckhouse. It tasted completely different to the other beers I'd tasted. It had greater depth and more taste nuances; it was more complex.

At the time, I had been on a student grant for a number of years and was used to having to make savings. So I thought maybe I could save a lot of money if I could brew a beer like that myself, i.e. if I could make 20 litres (5 gallons) for the price of a half... That was my motivation to start with, and I soon brought Keller in on the idea. At first, we tried out some beer kits that I'd purchased on the internet from a brewing shop in Vejle. But they were just syrup that you mixed with hot water and the final beer tasted awful.

After just six or seven brews, I got hold of some American books on brewing, and at the same time I e-mailed Allan Poulsen at Brøckhouse brewery. He was the person who had brewed the beer I had tasted at Plan B, and I was curious to know what ingredients he had used. Allan sent a friendly reply but didn't give me the whole recipe, so Keller and I set about trying to 'clone' Brøckhouse's IPA and gave our version the name Brauhaus IPA. It was made using an all-grain brewing method with real malt, hops and yeast. We stored all the ingredients and our brewing equipment in the basement, and once a week or so – usually at weekends – we went down and made our arms numb turning the handle of the grinding machine. The smell of malt and hops filled the staircase, but as we lived just around the corner from Carlsberg, we imagined the neighbours probably thought the smell was coming from there.

We got bottles for the beer from a SPAR shop in Frederiksberg Allé, where they had Brøckhouse bottles with stoppers at deposit price. We carefully cleaned and disinfected them at home in mine and Pernille's small kitchen before filling them and leaving the beer to stand and secondary ferment in wooden boxes on the floor. Proceeding by trial and error, we ended up making nine different versions of Brauhaus IPA. Then we adjusted it slightly as we went along by modifying the addition of hops and malt and using different brewing temperatures and yeast types. Attempting to clone the beer was a really good way to start because we discovered what happened if, for example, we boiled the beer for a little longer or slightly adjusted the caramel malt.

Our very first brew tasted reasonably good and we began serving the beer at BØF events. The only problem was that the members were all friends of ours, so we couldn't really expect them to taste our beer objectively. We therefore decided to subject Brauhaus IPA to a blind tasting to determine 'Denmark's best beer 2005'. Our beer won! So we thought, 'Okay, if the BØF members all like it, there must be others who'll like it too'. Consequently, we started brewing more.

THE BEER LEEKS

At that time, American microbrewing had already found its way to the Danish market in the form of hoppier, bitter beers from breweries such as Sierra Nevada, Anchor and Brooklyn Brewery, which in time we got round to tasting and found to be far more interesting than Brøckhouse's India Pale Ale. Most other breweries were making beers that tasted similar to Carlsberg but had fancier labels. That wasn't for us. It was more fun to make more extreme, high-flavour beers like those in the USA, so we began adding more hops and developing the recipes rather than just cloning.

Generally speaking, we weren't afraid to experiment, but every so often things didn't quite go to plan. One time, for example, we set about trying to brew a lambic at home in the kitchen in Vesterbro. In principle, it's a beer type that can only be brewed in the Payottenland region of Belgium because the mix of microorganisms found in the air there is particularly suitable for getting the beer to spontaneously ferment. But we simply left the buckets standing overnight on the window sill without any lids on.

The next day, we put lids on and dragged the buckets up to Keller's attic, where the beer was allowed to stand and ferment for the best part of a year. When it was time to bottle it, we obtained a 200-litre (53-gallon) wooden cask from the Belgian lambic brewery Cantillon and I got my friend Lasse to help drag it up to the attic. We hauled the 60- to 70-kilo(132-154lb)cask all the way up the stairs to the fourth floor, in through Keller's apartment and up the back stairs to the attic. But when we reached the attic, the door was just too narrow to get the cask in and we had to drag it all the way down again and get eight 30-litre (8-gallon) buckets that we could transfer the beer into. We then drove the buckets to our small storeroom in Valby, where we were finally able to transfer the lambic to the cask.

At this point, the beer began leaking out through the joints of the cask onto the concrete floor. In panic, we ran to a nearby kiosk and bought some bright-red strawberry chewing gum, which we hurriedly chewed so that we could seal up the joints with it. Not surprisingly, this didn't help one bit, so we drove to Silvan to get a silicone gun. Fortunately, by the time we got back, the beer had stopped leaking. The wood had become soaked and expanded, making the cask tight again, but we simply had no experience of that sort of thing back then.

A few years ago, we bottled some of the old lambic from the cask for the first time and served it with pork and sauerkraut at a beer lunch at the Mielcke & Hurtigkarl restaurant in Copenhagen. The beer turned out to be surprisingly good and not too dissimilar to a lambic from Belgium, proving that it is possible to make spontaneously fermented beer outside Payottenland.

DANISH CRAFT BREWING CHAMPIONS

I had been interested in Danish design for some time, especially Verner Panton's furniture and lamps, among others, and I helped the owner of a German vintage furniture shop in Stuttgart to track down much-sought-after Panton designs in Denmark. That's why there were Verner Panton patterns on our first labels. We printed them out ourselves and applied them to the bottles using milk. They stuck well, and it was easy to get them off again and wash the bottles clean afterwards.

We had also decided that our brewery should be called Mikkeller. It was actually a perfectly obvious name; a combination of Mikkel and Keller. One of the BØF members, Hans, also a brewer, had a girlfriend who was good at drawing and he had got her to draw a portrait of himself for his labels. We thought they looked really good, so we gave her a box of beers for drawing a picture of us. The drawing, in black and white, depicted us both in profile and was used as the logo on our new labels.

We also entered the Danish craft brewing championship. Every year, the winners of the competition were announced at the Danish Beer

TO ØL 8% BA SNOWBALL	40				7.7%
TO ØL 7% BA SANS FRONTIER	40	**39**	MIKKELLER 7.7%		
TO ØL BA MINE IS BIGGER THAN YOURS 12.5% MUSCATE	45	**40**	MIKKELLER 7.7%		

Enthusiasts' Beer Festival at the Valby Hallen concert venue in Copenhagen. Our eighth brew – the very first one not to be made using a kit but with real ingredients – won bronze medal in the Belgian tripel category. The same year, we won silver with a brown ale, and the year after gold.

In 2005, Jeppe and his friend Michael opened Ølbutikken (The Beer Shop) in Oehlenschlägergade, Copenhagen. Initially, Keller and I were involved in the plans to open a bar or a shop, but Jeppe and I were often falling out and, although we invariably made up again, it became increasingly clear that it wouldn't be a good idea to go into business together. However, Keller and I did brew a special beer for the opening, Ølbutikken IPA, and Jeppe and Michael began distributing our beer through the shop. I also worked there a few days a week, which meant I came into contact with lots of different beer lovers from both Denmark and abroad.

With the distribution through Ølbutikken, reviews of our beers began to appear on ratebeer.com, a forum for beer enthusiasts around the world who taste, review and swap beers through the site For example, a Dane might swap 20 beers with an American, so they both get 20 beers they haven't tried before. Some beers are worth more than others; a bottle of Dark Lord from the American brewery Three Floyds can be swapped for 20 'ordinary' beers. In this way, our beers were also being sent around the world, and beer geeks across the globe suddenly began to notice us, send us fan mail and inquire where they could buy our beers. The following year, when ratebeer.com declared Ølbutikken to be the world's best beer shop, people really began flocking to us.

BEER GEEK BREAKFAST

The beer with which we had most success was an oat stout. When it had fermented and was still in the tank, it actually tasted quite boring. It lacked something. I had the idea of adding coffee, so I wrote to a few brewers who I knew had added coffee to their beer asking how they did it. One was Anders Kissmeyer from Nørrebro Bryghus, who used a rather complicated process involving cold-water extract, which had to stand and infuse for many days. The Californian brewery AleSmith's process, however, was simplicity itself: 'Brew a press pot of coffee and pour it in'. We did that, and it completely changed the character of the beer, transforming it into a really good coffee stout.

At the end of 2005, this beer, christened Beer Geek Breakfast, was distributed through Ølbutikken. It received top ratings and in January 2006 was declared best stout in the world on ratebeer.com, while Mikkeller was declared the 37th best microbrewery out of 5,836. This really kick-started demand for our beer. At the time, we were only brewing around 50 litres (13 gallons) at a time at home in the kitchen and did not therefore have any beer to sell. We also had plans to have our first stand at the upcoming Beer Festival. So, we signed an agreement with the Danish microbreweries Andrik and Ørbæk to use their facilities when they were idle, allowing us to brew up to 2000 litres (528 gallons) of beer at a time.

Alongside the brewing, I was still working as a physics and maths teacher at Det frie Gymnasium, and Keller had got himself a job at the Ølfabrikken microbrewery in Holløselund and learnt to brew in a large-scale facility. He had a grasp of all the practical aspects of brewing, whilst I was responsible for coming up with the recipes. I could just about get my head around shovelling malt, but otherwise I had no real sense of brewing beer in such large quantities. My background as a physics and chemistry teacher was an advantage, however, because I had an understanding of the basic chemical processes. I knew, for example, what happens when starch is broken down into sugar. This made it easier to make small changes to the process and adjust each brew until it was just how we wanted it.

For the Beer Festival in Valby Hallen we had rented the smallest stand, and shared it with the Belgian microbrewery De Struise Brouwers, which at the time, was relatively unknown, just like us. On the stand we had gathered a small group of friends to help pour the nine different beers that we offered over the three days. During the festival, we also held meetings with two American distributors who, together with four others, had contacted us beforehand because they were interested in signing a contract with us. We had chosen the two that we thought had most to offer and ended up signing up with the Shelton Brothers firm. This was the start of our foreign exports.

MIKKEL/KELLER

Once again, we needed to increase our production and were unable to brew enough at Andrik and Ørbæk's facilities. We weren't interested in investing in our own brewery. If we'd had to borrow a large sum of money for equipment, we would have been forced to sell more and make more 'commercial' beer. We didn't want to do that. So, in autumn 2006, we contacted Gourmetbryggeriet in Roskilde, at the time one of the most well-established microbreweries in Denmark, and began to brew our beers there.

The following spring, the brewery's owners invited us to a meeting. They could see we were doing well, so they proposed expanding the partnership. They would produce Mikkeller's beer if, in return, they could become partners in the company. I had a really bad feeling about that and sensed that a partnership would mean that we lost control of the beer's quality – that it would become about brewing as much as possible as cheaply as possible and would mean an end to developing new recipes. We hadn't made more than five beers up to then, and I had tons of ideas. It was obviously great that we'd begun to make money, but it was more fun making beer. Keller, by contrast, was more open to the offer, and that caused friction between us. When I ended up vetoing the deal, Gourmetbryggeriet no longer had any space in their calendar for us, so suddenly we had nowhere to brew.

In the meantime, Keller had found a job as a writer for the music magazine Soundvenue and wasn't doing as much work for Mikkeller as me even though the tasks were multiplying. Suddenly, we had to deliver beers to bars and shops, whilst also doing the brewing and taking care of all the admin. So I began to run my own race. I decided

to contact the Belgian De Proef Brewery on the recommendation of another Danish brewery. This was a landmark moment because they had capacity and suddenly we had the opportunity to brew beer in very large quantities. De Proef's owner and brewer, Dirk Naudts, and I quickly realized that we were a good match; he had the technical know-how and I had the ideas.

In August 2007, Keller and I agreed that he would leave Mikkeller with half the profits from the previous year. Meanwhile, production and sales grew steadily and there was more and more work to be done at Mikkeller. I took care of everything: packed the export orders, delivered beer, handled VAT, duties, tax, the food authorities and the Dansk Retursystem (the Danish deposit and return system for bottles and cans), updated websites and got labels designed. I was also marking maths assignments and teaching at the school. I worked from six o'clock in the morning until midnight day-in day-out. At that time, Pernille had a full-time job with a newspaper and we hardly saw each other, living almost parallel lives. This was unsustainable in the long term, and when I found out in spring 2008 that I was going to be a father, I had to make some changes. I did that by hiring my first employee, Thomas, who was mad about beer and was writing a thesis on Mikkeller at the IT University. As part of the thesis, he managed our website and began making short, funny handheld videos that he posted on the site. They soon became extremely popular in beer circles and helped create Mikkeller's image as an uncompromising, rebellious company.

When Thomas completed his thesis, he began delivering beer and taking care of all sorts of other tasks. I had switched to part-time at the school, but it still became increasingly dissatisfying being a teacher. I was unable to build up a good relationship with the pupils or to engage properly with my work. Having said that, I liked teaching and didn't want to give up my colleagues and the team element for the prospect of sitting alone in my office at home. However, with beer production and sales increasing dramatically from 2008 to 2009, the following year I took the leap and gave up teaching completely.

Since then, Mikkeller has grown steadily. Today, I travel the world meeting importers and attending beer festivals, giving lectures and conducting beer tastings. My beer is brewed at microbreweries in Belgium, Norway and the USA, among others, and exported to more than 40 countries all over the world. Furthermore, Mikkeller has opened four bars: two in Copenhagen, one in San Francisco and one in Bangkok. Every day, I can be found in an open-plan office in Vesterbro, Copenhagen, with my ten permanent employees.

Beer has thus become a business for me, but I still find it fun coming up with new recipes and, most of all, tasting the results. With running and other things I've devoted myself to over time, there has been a natural boundary where I could not go any further – where the possibilities were exhausted. But the beer world is vast, and I still get lots of new ideas for new projects and new beer.

It can happen when I'm drinking yuzu juice whilst I have a salt liquorice in my mouth, or when we mix the remnants of a cherry wine with a stout purely for fun during a break at the office. And, not least, when I head out to meet foreign brewers, chefs and other people who are crazy about what they do.

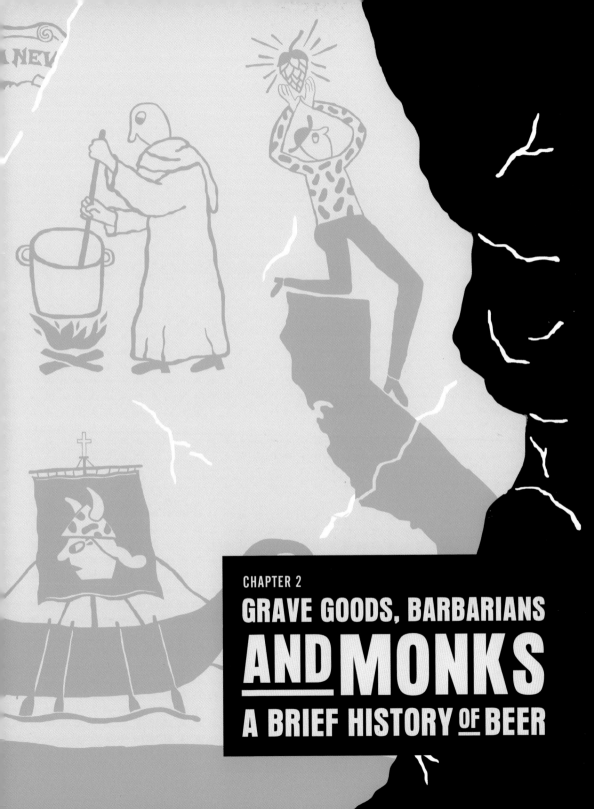

CHAPTER 2
GRAVE GOODS, BARBARIANS
AND MONKS
A BRIEF HISTORY OF BEER

Noah carried it on the Ark, Elizabeth I drank it for breakfast, and the Egyptians took it with them to the grave. There are many stories and myths surrounding beer, but the facts are that this fermented drink has been brewed for the best part of 8000 years – as long as cereals have been routinely cultivated – and had a variety of forms and functions along the way.

In ancient times, beer was a porridge-like substance made from crushed-up, yeasty bread. One of the first sources of evidence of brewing dates back to the holy city of Nippur in Sumer, Mesopotamia, which was founded in 5000 BC. Here, legend has it that the beer goddess Ninkasa brewed beer, regarded as a holy drink, for the temples. In ancient Egypt, beer was the most common drink, consumed in large quantities by, among others, thirsty pyramid builders. Beer and brewing methods are discussed in detail in offering lists and on grave reliefs from 2900 BC.

Together with the knowledge of cereal cultivation, beer brewing spread from the Middle East to the Mediterranean and on to Germany and Northern Europe. In the Roman Empire, beer became the drink of the masses, while the higher classes drank wine and looked down on the drinking habits of the Germanic barbarians. In Northern and Eastern Europe, beer was a normal part of every household, with each family drinking around one litre (33fl oz) a day of the nutritious beverage. Consumption increased significantly through the Middle Ages and the Renaissance, which represented the golden age of beer when both rich and poor drank it all day long. Given the salty food and lack of clean drinking water, it was not uncommon for adults to quench their thirst with six litres (1½ gallons) a day. Fermentation occurred spontaneously, and the beer, dark in colour and low in alcohol, was flavoured and preserved with a mixture of berries and aromatic plants.

Home-brewed beer was a common means of paying church taxes, and generally speaking beer was a matter for the clergy, who set specific requirements for strength and taste. A priest was ill-regarded if he did not drink beer, and monks in abbeys produced beer both to make money and to drink while fasting. In the Nordic region, beer was an important drink in Viking times, regularly cropping up in the sagas of Nordic mythology. In Denmark, the earliest evidence of beer is found in the grave of the Egtved Girl, which has been dated to 1370 BC, the middle of the Bronze Age. As in the rest of Europe, brewing subsequently became an important and widespread feature of the farming culture.

At the start of the 1800s, the technological advances of the Industrial Revolution ushered in new methods and standards for brewing. In Denmark, Carlsberg founder J.C. Jacobsen began systematically brewing beer in 1847, breaking with the home-brewing tradition by adopting scientific methodology. Inspired by Bavarian traditions, Jacobsen created bottom-fermented, long-stored beer, and when in 1883 Carlsberg researcher Emil Christian Hansen succeeded in cultivating pure yeast, the Carlsberg empire was assured and the seeds of large-scale global production of lager beer were sown. The development of pure yeast and modern laboratory methods revolutionized brewing as we know it today. It created the platform for the dominance of bottom-fermented beers, thereby decimating production of top-fermented beers and, for the most part, eradicating them from small brewhouses and pubs in post-war Europe and the USA.

Brewing giants such as Carlsberg, Budweiser and Heineken set the standard well into the 1990s until the microbrewing revolution really took hold and changed the European and American perception of beer.

CHAPTER 3

MICROBREWING & THE BEER REVOLUTION

Mikkeller's story is both an individual story of hops, endeavour and ambition, and the story of a broader trend in which the small Danish brewery became caught up at the start of the twenty-first century, namely the beer revolution that had started on the other side of the North Sea and also across the Atlantic as far back as the 1970s.

It all began with a consumer revolution in the British Isles. One day in March 1971, four young Englishmen were enjoying a beer at Kruger's Bar in the Irish village of Dunquin. The economic slump in post-war England had given brewing giants such as Whitbread and Guinness far too much latitude, and the four friends were fed up with tasteless mass-produced beer. Keen to revitalize beer in their home country, they resolved to start up a consumer organization, and the Campaign for the Revitalisation of Real Ale was duly born.

In the following years, membership of this grass-roots movement steadily grew, and in 1973 it was renamed CAMRA (Campaign for Real Ale). CAMRA purposefully set about promoting quality beer and protecting small breweries, pubs and consumer rights. In the subsequent decades, CAMRA's message spread to other parts of the world, where local branches and similar organizations sprouted up.

At the start of the 1970s, craft brewers on the west coast of the USA also began stirring. One of them was John 'Jack' McAuliffe. Sent to Scotland with the US navy at the end of the 1960s, McAuliffe had acquired a taste for British pale ales and lagers that he took home with him to San Francisco. A few years previously, in 1965, Fritz Maytag, the wealthy heir to a washing machine empire, had sat down at a bar in San Francisco and ordered his favourite beer, an Anchor Steam. The bar owner had tipped him off about the Anchor Steam Brewery, which at that time was on the verge of bankruptcy. If San Francisco's Bay Area was to avoid being dominated by Budweiser, something had to be done, so the next day Maytag bought a 51% shareholding in the small brewery, which he then purchased outright four years later. McAuliffe found inspiration in Maytag's Anchor Steam Brewery to start up his own microbrewery, New Albion Brewing. This operation opened in Sonoma, California, in October 1976, and in the six and a bit years of its lifetime it succeeded in inspiring a plethora of imitators, including Ken Grossman.

As a child, Grossman had been taught home-brewing by a friend's father, and in 1976 he opened a store in the Northern Californian town of Chico, selling home-brewing equipment. Under McAuliffe's expert guidance, he then developed his own brewery together with his business partner Paul Camusi. He called it Sierra Nevada Brewing. At the time, American home-brewers found it difficult to obtain good-quality hops. Consequently, Grossman drove all the way from Chico to Yakima, Washington, to buy hops directly from local dealers. He returned with whole hop cones in his luggage, and in 1980 he and Camusi began brewing their world-famous well-hopped Sierra Nevada Pale Ale using home-built equipment and discarded German copper kettles. The beer acquired iconic status in American beer history and inspired a wealth of Grossman and Camusi imitators to make their own pale ales.

The three above-mentioned Californian breweries – Anchor Brewing Company, New Albion Brewing Company and Sierra Nevada Brewing – became the biggest pioneers of the American microbrewing movement that exploded in the following decades. In the 30 years from 1965, the number of American microbreweries multiplied five-fold, and American farmers began meeting the microbrewers' need for high-quality hops by expanding cultivation of local varieties, such as Cascade, Amarillo and Chinook, and coming up with new varieties by crossing different varieties of older origin. All this helped make the Americans microbrewers' interpretations of British pale ales and India Pale Ales more extreme and powerful in taste as they acquired the characteristic notes of citrus and grape.

Another country that played an important role in the evolution of microbrewing was Belgium. Long before the beer revolution started in Great Britain and the USA, small traditional Belgian Trappist breweries such as Chimay, Westvleteren and Orval had been brewing versatile top-fermented ales that differed significantly from the generally well-known bottom-fermented lagers. During the 1990s, the Trappist monks' brewing began drawing attention outside the country's borders and, together with CAMRA and the newly arisen Californian micro-breweries, came to form the main arteries in the flow of microbrewed beer, which in the coming decades slowly spread to the rest of the world, inspiring countless home-brewers to challenge the beer giants and causing consumers to make increasing demands of beer quality.

PROBABLY THE BEST BEER IN THE WORLD

American pale ales, such as Sierra Nevada and Anchor, and Belgian Trappist beers finally found their way onto the Danish market at the end of the 1990s. This happened after the Danish counterpart to CAMRA, Danske Ølentusiaster (Danish Beer Enthusiasts), was founded in 1998 by a small group of beer lovers. Two of them, Anders Evald and Søren Houmøller, were actually members of a small wine club, but a series of work trips to Brussels made them aware of Trappist beer. They decided to found the beer club KØLIG (a Danish acronym for 'Club for Beer-Loving Folk'), and alongside the club started small-scale garage sales of exclusive imported beers. Through their website they made contact with Unibank's beer club The Four Seasons and the craft brewer Ole Madsen, and together they started Danske Ølentusiaster.

Like the founders of CAMRA, these beer lovers were fed up with factory-made beer, which in Denmark is synonymous with Carlsberg and Tuborg. They wanted to put basic quality craft back into beer and challenge the Danish national consensus by questioning the Carlsberg slogan 'Probably the best beer in the world'. With their, at the time, controversial message and their constructive criticism of Carlsberg's and Tuborg's 'uninteresting' beer, Danske Ølentusiaster succeeded in spreading the message in the Danish media. The association's first beer festival, held at Remisen in Østerbro, Copenhagen, in 2001, raised interest in, and hence demand for, foreign microbrewed beer.

This whetted the appetite of Danish home-brewers. One of the first was IT consultant Allan Poulsen from Gribskov. Since 1995, Poulsen had been brewing at home in his cellar and had even built a 40-litre (10½-gallons) copper system with which he made beers including Brøckhouse IPA. This ale received the award of 'New Beer of the Year' at the 2002 Danske Ølentusiaster festival.

Another person tired of machine-made characterless beer was former Carlsberg brewer Anders Kissmeyer. In 2003, Kissmeyer opened the ambitious Nørrebro Brewery in Ryesgade. As well as a large open-brewing facility, the brewery houses a restaurant where the food is intended to accompany the beer and not vice versa. In Denmark, this helped to turn the focus onto beer as a more cultivated beverage that can be enjoyed with food other than breadsticks and hot dogs.

From 2005 to 2008, microbreweries popped up across the country. In all, 71 breweries opened as, paradoxically, beer sales in Denmark declined (partly explained by increasing beer purchases south of the border in Germany). But consumers were increasingly demanding quality rather than quantity, and the microbreweries provided authenticity and story-telling. Brewmasters, who previously had been anonymous, came into the foreground and helped profile their own brands.

The supermarket Irma, resturant Mad & Vin i Magasin plus department stores and a number of specialist stores began selling microbrewed beer, and beer became an integral part of the gourmet culture that arose during the economic upturn of the 2000s; it became something that people were happy to spend a lot of money on. At the same time, beer enthusiasts from all around the world established their own networks through social media and began hyping different beers and breweries, not least by reviewing them on ratebeer.com. In this way, new types of beer found their way into student culture, which began to replace boxes of discount beer with microbrewed beer presented in champagne bottles.

During 2007, a new brewery was opening every month, but many were aiming for mass appeal and brewing beers that were not particularly distinctive. This had consequences when the financial crisis hit. Allan Poulsen's Brøckhouse, for example, which in that year brewed a full 600,000 litres (158,503 gallons) of beer, called time on the business just two years later along with a number of other Danish breweries that had invested millions in advanced stainless steel brewing equipment. Some 58% of the breweries that made it through the crisis unscathed had either secured good agreements with supermarket chains such as Coop and Irma (Bryggeriet Skands and Nørrebro Bryghus) or had good local support (Braunstein in Køge and Thisted Bryghus). Fortunately, Mikkeller had a firm foothold in the foreign market and chose to focus on exports. There were no other Danish microbreweries that made the breakthrough internationally in the same way.

In spite of economic adversity, the microbrewing revolution left the Danish and international beer scene changed forever and permanently altered the perception of the golden nectar. Today, beer is no longer drunk simply to quench thirst or induce drunkenness. It is a beverage that is treated with respect, care and no little reverence by beer lovers the world over.

CHAPTER 4

PALE, BITTER, DARK, SOUR

BEER TYPES

WITH HUNDREDS OF DIFFERENT BEER TYPES AND MANY VARIATIONS WITHIN EACH ONE, IT CAN BE A TRICKY BUSINESS DEFINING ONE PARTICULAR STYLE. JUST AS MUSIC GENRES OR ART MOVEMENTS ARE ROUTINELY REINTERPRETED AND TURNED ON THEIR HEAD, SO TOO BEER TYPES MAY HAVE DIFFERENT CHARACTERISTICS DEPENDING ON WHERE IN THE WORLD THEY COME FROM OR HOW THEY'VE BEEN CREATED. IT IS WORTHWHILE, THOUGH, TO CARRY OUT A GENERAL CLASSIFICATION OF SOME OF THE MOST IMPORTANT BEER TYPES.

PALE/MILD BEERS

PILSNER

P ilsner lager is the best known and most common beer type in the world. It was first brewed by the German-born brewer Josef Groll in 1842 in the town of Plzeň (Pilsen) in the west of what is now the Czech Republic. Groll was inspired by a Bavarian brewing method that used yeast that was active at low temperatures because, for reasons of hygiene, the beer was aged and stored in cellars. The yeast settled at the bottom of the fermentation tank and was therefore referred to as bottom-fermenting yeast.

A typical pilsner lager is clear and light-yellow to golden in colour with an alcohol content of approximately 4–5% abv (alcohol by volume, i.e. volume percentage). Czech pilsner generally contains the by-product diacetyl, which gives the beer a fuller, almost buttery taste. Diacetyl can occur during fermentation and is generally regarded as an unwanted off-flavour, but it can also be a by-product for which the brewer deliberately strives.

MIKKEL'S RECOMMENDATIONS

Mikkeller
American Dream
Vesterbro Pilsner

Emerson's
Pilsner

To Øl
Raid Beer

Plzeňský Prazdroj
Pilsner Urqell

„„ MIKKEL'S NOTES

Pilsner is a bottom-fermented beer brewed at lower temperatures, so the yeast does not generally taste as strong. This makes it easier to bring out the flavour of the other ingredients in the beer to create a cleaner impression, but it also means that lagers are generally not particularly varied. Technically then, it is more difficult to brew a good lager than, for example, a good pale ale because any errors that occur during the brewing process are easily tasted.

WEISSBIER

(WHEAT BEER)

Weissbier (wheat beer) originates from Germany and contains a high proportion of pale wheat malt (around 60%) in relation to barley. Wheat contains a number of proteins that contribute to a rich head and give the beer a characteristic cloudy appearance.

Weissbier also bears the stamp of esters and phenols, aromatic substances that are produced during fermentation and give the weissbier its banana-like notes. Generally 4–6% abv in strength.

,, MIKKEL'S NOTES

Contrary to popular belief, weissbier gets its taste from its yeast and not from its wheat. It is a very traditional beer style developed over many years. It is difficult to work with because it quickly loses its distinctive characteristics. If, for example, you add more hops, it starts tasting like an IPA. This makes it a highly predictable and reliable beer type, but – in my view – that also makes it a rather boring style.

MIKKEL'S RECOMMENDATIONS

Maisel
Weisse original

Weihenstephan
Hefe Weissbier

WITBIER

Like weissbier (wheat beer), witbier, which originates from Belgium, is brewed with large amounts of pale wheat. Unlike weissbier, however, witbier is brewed with unmalted wheat, which gives this beer type a paler, semi-cloudy appearance.

Witbier is a descendant of Belgian medieval beers, which were produced without hops. In order to preserve and spice the beer, brewers instead used *gruit* – a mix of herbs and spices. A modern witbier has added coriander and dried orange peel, which give the beer a characteristic freshness and spicy taste. In Denmark, witbier made something of a breakthrough in Danish cafes and bars at the start of the 2000s with the Belgian 'Hoegaarden'. Generally 4–7% abv.

🗩🗩 MIKKEL'S NOTES

A witbier is very similar to a weissbier, but it is easier to experiment with because it has a lighter, fresher character that can tolerate the addition of various hops and spices. You can also modify the alcohol content without the beer losing its 'wit' character.

SAISON

MIKKEL'S RECOMMENDATIONS

Mikkeller
Saison Sally

**Anchorage
Brewing Company**
Love Buzz

Brasserie Dupont
Avec les Bons Voeux

'**S**aison' is French for 'season'. The designation refers to beer that was originally brewed in the winter months on farms in the French-speaking region of Belgium, Wallonia, and drunk by peasants in the fields in the summer. Modern saison beer is fermented at a very high temperature, which produces a lot of taste nuances in the beer. Saison beer is pale and spicy with an alcohol content of around 5–8% abv. In the USA, this rustic beer style has enjoyed a renaissance in the form of 'farmhouse ales'.

❞ MIKKEL'S NOTES

Saison is an exciting style because you can push the yeast to its limits when you expose it to very high temperatures. This makes it difficult to control but fun to experiment with, because the results are unpredictable. Saison is also one of the few pale beer types that is worth barrel-aging.

SMOKED BEER

MIKKEL'S RECOMMENDATIONS

Mikkeller
Beer Geek Bacon
Rauchpils

Ölvisholt Brugghús
Lava

Aecht Schlenkerla
Fastenbier

S moked beer has added smoked malt which permeates the beer. Any beer type brewed with smoked malt can be called a smoked beer. Historically, all malt was smoked over an open fire, as there were no other methods for drying it, but after the Industrial Revolution, brewers acquired new methods for heat-treating malt. This generally put a stop to the smoked beer style, although smoked beer continued to be brewed in certain places, especially Bamberg in Germany, which is famous for its *rauchbier*, Aecht Schlenkerla. A modern smoked beer can be brewed using different variations of smoked malt.

🗩🗩 MIKKEL'S NOTES

This is obviously a category with no limits, as brewers can work with smoke in any style of beer. You can give a beer a subtle, almost anonymous smokiness or use up to 100% smoked malt from the most extreme whisky distillery on the Isle of Islay in Scotland. As a rule, I'm not particularly fond of smoke in beer, which makes it even more challenging for me to achieve a balance with which I'm satisfied.

SESSION BEER

MIKKEL'S RECOMMENDATIONS

Mikkeller
Drink'in the Sun
Drink'in the Snow

Evil Twin
Bikini Beer

After a number of years focusing on extremely strong barrel-aged beers, microbrewers around the world have begun moving in the other direction and experimenting with beer that has relatively low alcohol content. A session beer is characterized by an alcohol content of maximum 5% abv and a balanced ratio of hops to malt, which makes it easy to drink. You can thus enjoy several session beers in succession without the taste buds being bombarded or ending up under the table.

MIKKEL'S NOTES

This category of beer is in many ways the opposite of 'extreme beer'. But in some ways it is not. Because if you can make a 0% abv beer that tastes like a good 5% abv pale ale, I would call that a very extreme beer. It is a huge challenge making alcohol-free beer that tastes good; it's like having a good burger without beef. I worked for more than two years on developing Mikkeller's alcohol-free beer 'Drink'in the Sun' by experimenting with yeasts that had never before been used in beer. That's the longest I've ever worked on a single beer.

BITTER

PALE ALE

MIKKEL'S RECOMMENDATIONS

Mikkeller
K:rlekserien
All Others Pale

To Øl
Nørrebro Pale Ale

Oskar Blues Brewery
Dale's Pale Ale

Three Floyds
Zombie Dust

Pale ale originated at the start of the 1700s in England, where it was a status symbol for the respectable middle classes, by contrast with darker brown ale, which was very much for the working classes. The beer type acquired its name because it is brewed with pale ale malt, a type that is dried at relatively low temperatures and therefore takes on a fairly pale colour. Pale ale is no darker than a lager and varies in colour from golden to golden-brown. Modern pale ales, developed in the USA in the 1970s and 1980s, are characterized by their bitterness and pronounced citrus notes that stem from American hops. Generally 4–6% abv.

🔖 MIKKEL'S NOTES

It was the pale ale Sierra Nevada that opened my eyes to American microbrewing at the end of the 1990s. To this very day, I think this beer is the perfect introduction to microbrewing because it is not extreme in character but still tastes good. Generally, this beer type is easy to introduce to less hardened beer enthusiasts. Quite simply, most people like pale ales. It is also a beer type that is fun to brew because there are untold possibilities in terms of the hops.

TOP-FERMENTED BEER

Top-fermented beer ferments at high temperatures (generally 18-22°C/64-71°F). In the process, the yeast collects in a thick layer on top of the liquid. A top-fermented beer ferments quickly – in just 3-6 days. This type of beer often has yeast residues at the bottom of the bottle and is cloudy. The broad designation for this type of beer is 'ale'.

BOTTOM-FERMENTED BEER

By contrast to top-fermented beer, bottom-fermented beer ferments slowly – in 1-3 weeks – at low temperatures (generally 11-12°C/50-53°F). The yeast collects at the bottom of the fermentation tank and is easy to remove from the beer. Bottom-fermented beer is therefore usually clear. The broad designation for this type of beer is 'lager'.

SPONTANEOUSLY FERMENTED BEER

This is the oldest form of beer. Instead of adding yeast to the wort, the brewer leaves the tun open so that the wort is 'infected' by natural yeast and bacteria in the air. Consequently, the fermentation, and hence the taste of the beer, is dependent on the composition of the microorganisms that are found in the air.

INDIA PALE ALE (IPA)

0

According to a now well-known anecdote concerning the origin of IPA, the British brewer George Hodgson invented this beer type at the end of the 1700s. Hodgson was tasked with transporting a beer by ship to the British colonies in India, and in order to make the beer more resilient to the long trip, he added extra hops and increased the alcohol content. He also stored it in oak barrels, which reportedly caused the beer to develop a particular complexity and bitterness that proved extremely popular. Like ordinary pale ale, the IPA was subsequently refined by brewers on the American west coast, where it acquired its characteristic bitterness and fruity aroma from American hops. An IPA is generally slightly darker than an ordinary pale ale – from dark-golden to amber-red with an alcohol content of 6–8% abv.

A variation of IPA is imperial IPA (IIPA) or double IPA, which signifies an IPA with a higher alcohol content and more hops. If you just use a single hop variety in an IPA, it is referred to as a single-hop IPA.

MIKKEL'S RECOMMENDATIONS

Mikkeller
Green Gold
Single Hop IPA-series
Crooked Moon Tattoo dIPA
I Beat yoU

Surly
Overrated West Coast IPA

AleSmith
IPA

Russian River
Pliny the Elder

Three Floyds
Dreadnaught

MIKKEL'S NOTES

It was an India pale ale that got me started in brewing. For the first time, I experienced how the hop was the focus of the beer, which could taste fresh and flowery. The possibilities within India Pale Ales are unlimited because there are so many markedly different hop varieties and because this is a world undergoing constant development as new hop types continually come into being. Consequently, this is also the beer type that we have brewed most at Mikkeller.

FRESH HOP ALE

F resh hop ales – also called wet hop ales – are top-fermented beers to which only completely fresh hops are added. The beer type is only brewed once a year during the hop harvest. Every October, the world's largest hop-producing region, Yakima in Washington, USA, holds its Fresh Hop Festival after the harvest has taken place. All the beers featured in the festival must be brewed with hops that make the transition from field to beer within 24 hours.

Fresh hop ales are mainly brewed on the American west coast and are generally used in well-hopped beer types such as pale ales and India pale ales.

MIKKEL'S RECOMMENDATIONS

Great Divide
Fresh Hop Pale Ale

Surly
Wet

Sierra Nevada
Harvest Ale

,, MIKKEL'S NOTES

This beer type is difficult to brew in Europe because, in my opinion, European hop varieties are not particularly suitable for brewing beer when freshly harvested. We have tried a few times, but the result has been somewhat underwhelming.

BROWN ALE

In 18th-century Britain, the term brown ale was used as a general designation for beer brewed with brown malt that took on a corresponding brown colour. In the 20th century, large breweries such as Scottish & Newcastle and Whitbread enjoyed success with their versions of brown ales. Like many other beer types of English origin, brown ale was reinterpreted by American brewers in the 1980s in a stronger, hoppier version. American brown ales generally have caramel and chocolate notes from the roasted malt, and are moderately bitter, with an alcohol content of around 3–7% abv.

❞❞ MIKKEL'S NOTES

You could call a brown ale a hybrid of a porter and a pale ale. This makes it interesting to brew because you can take the best from both worlds. When Keller and I won gold at the Danish craft brewing championship, it was with a brown ale.

MIKKEL'S RECOMMENDATIONS

Mikkeller
Jackie Brown

Cigar City
Maduro Brown Ale

The Kernel
India Brown Ale

STOUT/PORTER

MIKKEL'S RECOMMENDATIONS

Mikkeller
Beer Geek Breakfast
Texas Ranger
Milk Stout

Three Floyds
Moloko Plus

St. James's Gate
Guinness

In the world of beer, opinion is divided about the difference between porter and stout. Porter was so named because it was first brewed as a more nourishing beer for the port workers in 19th century England. The word stout, on the other hand, signifying 'robust' or 'solid', was later used for a stronger porter. Regardless of the name, this dark beer is often characterized by a rich, mellow taste with coffee, chocolate or nut notes from the dark-roasted malt or barley. It ranges in alcohol content from 4% to 8% abv, and the bitterness is generally moderate. Within the stout category, there are also variations such as dry stout – the Irish version (for example, Guinness) which, in spite of the dark colour, is characterized by being refreshing and light with a low alcohol content of 3–5% abv. Another variation is milk stout, which has lactose added during fermentation.

,, MIKKEL'S NOTES

This type of beer has a special place in my heart because it was a stout, 'Beer Geek Breakfast', that sparked the whole Mikkeller adventure. Many people regard stouts and porters as a heavy, strong and difficult-to-drink beer type, but today you can make many different types of stout with every conceivable ingredient, such as oats, coffee, fruits, chilli, vanilla, etc. In this way, you can modify the character of the beer and make it much more complex.

IMPERIAL STOUT

MIKKEL'S RECOMMENDATIONS

Mikkeller
Beer Geek Brunch Weasel
George

AleSmith
Speedway Stout

Cigar City
Hunahpu's Imperial Stout

The term 'imperial stout' or 'Russian imperial stout' was originally used to describe the stout that the British exported to the Russian court in the 19th century. In order to preserve the beer on the long journey by ship, it was brewed with a higher alcohol content. In modern imperial stouts, the high alcohol content is balanced out by intensifying the bitterness, the sweetness or both. Imperial stouts are always dark, with a high alcohol content, from around 9% right up to 18% abv. Within the past three years, freeze-distillation of strong beers has gained in prominence, allowing beers with an alcohol content in excess of 50% abv.

,, MIKKEL'S NOTES

If you look at ratebeer's top 50, you will see that imperial stouts are generally extremely popular with beer geeks. This is due to this particular beer style being able to withstand the most extreme experimentation due to a high alcohol content and strong flavour. You can also age it in any type of barrel, and there are always new things to try. By way of example, I've tried boiling an imperial stout for 24 hours to obtain an almost tar-like consistency and then adding heaps of vanilla to give the beer a cake-like taste. This couldn't be done with any other beer type.

SOUR BEERS

LAMBIC
SPONTANEOUSLY FERMENTED BEER

Lambic is a spontaneously fermented beer type with no added yeast. Instead, it is exposed to bacteria and wild yeast spores in the air, which initiate fermentation. This fermentation method gives lambic a characteristic sour, vinous taste with the particular stamp of the *Brettanomyces* yeast strain. *Brettanomyces* is usually described as a mouldy, barnyardy or leathery taste that can be as undesirable in other beer types and traditional wines as it is sought after in lambic. Lambic originates from Payottenland in Belgium, where the air is reputed to have a unique composition of microorganisms. In recent years, however, brewers have also begun to experiment with spontaneously fermented beer in other parts of the world. A variation of lambic is gueuze, a blend of young and old lambic. Lambic often has fruit added, in which case the product takes it name from the fruit in question. Kriek (cherry) and framboise (raspberry) are the most common versions.

MIKKEL'S RECOMMENDATIONS

Mikkeller
Spontan Cherry
  Frederiksdal
Spontansauternes
Vesterbro Spontanale

Drie Fonteinen
Framboos

Girardin
Black Label Gueuze

🗩🗩 MIKKEL'S NOTES

Spontaneously fermented beer is the most exciting and unique beer style to brew because so much is left to chance. It takes several years for the beer to develop in the barrel, and it is exciting to monitor and taste it along the way. It is without doubt also the beer type that I most like to drink because you can taste the fact that it has been aging in barrels for years and had the time to develop a special complexity. At the same time, it is a beer style that is very difficult to introduce to novices because its particular sourness can be overwhelming at first.

SOUR ALE

MIKKEL'S RECOMMENDATIONS

Mikkeller
Årh Hvad?!
It's Alive

Rodenbach
Grand Cru

As its name implies, a sour ale tastes sour like a lambic but, unlike a lambic, it is fermented with a traditional ale yeast and only then does it get a mix of lactic acid bacteria and wild yeast added. Unlike sour ales, wild ales are not necessarily sour. A subcategory of sour ales is wild ales, which are often paler and have *Brettanomyces* added. Unlike sour ales, wild ales are not necessarily sour.

❞ MIKKEL'S NOTES

Sour ales are less exciting to brew than lambics because the fermentation is controlled. For the same reason, you do not obtain the same level of complexity in the beer. You could say that a sour ale tastes slightly more agreeable than a lambic.

Generally speaking, beer should always be stored in the cold and dark. Dark bottles in themselves serve as protection for the beer, and cans are actually even better because they protect against both sunlight and oxygen, which can cause unwanted off flavours in the beer. For the same reason, cans are becoming more and more popular as packaging with microbrewers, despite having been for many years synonymous with discount products. At the same time, they are easier to pack and more energy-saving to produce than glass bottles.

Ideally, beer should be stored at 12°C (53°F) like wine. The most important thing is to avoid movement and major temperature fluctuations. A well-hopped beer should be stored at lower tempe-ratures, as cold stops the fermentation process and prevents beer from aging too quickly.

STORAGE

BERLINER WEISSE

SOUR BEERS

As the name indicates, Berliner Weisse comes from Berlin. It goes all the way back to the 1600s, and at the end of the 1800s it was the most popular alcoholic drink in the German city. A modern Berliner Weisse has a low alcohol content – around 3% abv – and during the brewing process is exposed to lactic acid bacteria, to give it a sour character.

In Berlin, this beer type is often served with a small cup of green Waldmeister (woodruff) syrup or red raspberry syrup, which is poured in before the beer is drunk.

MIKKEL'S NOTES

Berliner Weisse is the new kid on the block. Just a few years ago, no one outside Berlin was brewing Berliner Weisse, but suddenly everyone is giving it a go. As with session beer, the challenge is to brew with a low alcohol content and still get some taste into the beer. With the modern versions, the syrup accompaniment is omitted, and brewers have begun adding berries during the brewing process instead.

MIKKEL'S RECOMMENDATIONS

The Kernel
London Sour

Professor Fritz Briem
1809 Berliner Style Weisse

Brodies
London Sour
   (Peach Edition)

BEER TYPES • 67

STRONG BEERS

BARLEY WINE

MIKKEL'S RECOMMENDATIONS

Mikkeller
French Oak Series

Mikkeller/Three Floyds
Boogoop

Barley wine is first and foremost characterized by its high alcohol content, which is close to that of wine. Reputedly, this strong beer originated in Britain during the Napoleonic Wars, when British gentlemen considered it unpatriotic to drink French wine and found a suitable alternative in strong beers. Other sources report, however, that this strong beer only replaced wine because wine imports stopped. Barley wine has an alcohol content of around 8–12% abv, is usually dark-golden or reddish in colour and has a rich, very sweet vinous character reminiscent of port or dessert wine. It is often barrel-aged.

🟥🟥 MIKKEL'S NOTES

Barley wine is an exciting beer style because during brewing you have a lot of freedom in terms of ingredients and alcohol. At the same time, you can put a lot of different traits into the beer by using different types of cereal. This is also a beer type that is well suited to barrel-aging.

DUBBEL
TRIPEL
QUADRUPEL

In the beer world, there are many different interpretations of the terms dubbel, tripel and quadrupel. The most common is that the trio of beer types, which stem from the Flemish-speaking region of Belgium and the Netherlands, were originally named based on how many barrels of malt were used in the brewing process. The more barrels of malt, the higher the alcohol content. Consequently, the rule of thumb today is that a tripel is stronger than a dubbel and a quadrupel is stronger than a tripel.

The red-brown **DUBBEL** or 'double' is one of the Trappist abbeys' most popular beer types and, with its dry sweetness and fruity notes, one of the easiest to recognize. Dubbel, as we know it today, was defined by the brewer Henrik Verlinden at the Westmalle brewery in 1926 and has an alcohol content of 6.5–8% abv.

By contrast to dubbel, **TRIPEL** is pale, a bit like a cloudy lager, but with a higher alcohol content of around 8–10%abv. It also has the complex, slightly spicy stamp of esters and phenols. Like dubbel, tripel is associated with the Belgian Trappist brewery Westmalle, where the beer type was named in 1956. It was created, however, in the 1930s.

QUADRUPEL has an alcohol content of 9–14% abv, making it the king of the Belgian beer family. It is characterized by its deep amber-red colour and notes of dried fruits such as figs, prunes or raisins. One of the world's most talked-about beers is a quadrupel, namely Westvleteren 12, brewed by the monks at the Saint-Sixtus Abbey in Westvleteren. On several occasions it has been declared the world's best and is a permanent fixture in the top five at ratebeer.com. It has an almost mythical reputation among beer geeks, partly due to the monks' anti-commercial sales methods, which mean that the beer can only be purchased at the abbey gate.

⟩⟩ MIKKEL'S NOTES

These beer types are defined on the basis of a long, highly traditional brewing culture in Belgium. It is therefore hard to be innovative with them. If you say 'quadrupel', anyone who knows anything about beer immediately connects it with the legendary Trappist brewery Westvleteren. It is difficult to work with and generally impossible to add anything new without moving away from the style. Apart from that, personally I could not bring myself to drink a quadrupel that is not from Belgium.

MIKKEL'S RECOMMENDATIONS

Mikkeller
Belgian Tripel
Monk's Elixir
Santa's Little Helper

Westmalle
Dubbel

Westvleteren
12

De Dolle Brouwers
Dulle Teve

Brasserie Rochefort
10

BARREL-AGED BEERS

BARREL-AGED BEERS

T his category includes any beer that is kept in wooden barrels for a prolonged period with the result that the beer takes on flavour from the wood or whatever has been kept in the barrel beforehand. Barrels that have previously held bourbon, whisky, wine or brandy are most commonly used. The barrel-aging process gives beers an extra complexity. Most dark and strong beer types are suitable for the barrel-aging process.

🗩🗩 MIKKEL'S NOTES

Barrel-aging provides untold possibilities for modifying or adding something to a beer. At the same time, a wooden barrel allows oxidation, so the beer ages completely differently to if it were kept in steel tanks. Furthermore, the whole wide world of spirits and wine can be brought into play in the beer world by deploying used barrels – from tequila and Grand Marnier to much vaunted white-wine barrels – which offer enormous potential. By way of example, we tried putting George, an imperial stout, in Cognac barrels and letting the wood and oxidation do their work on the beer for a whole year. It turned out to be a really good beer.

MIKKEL'S RECOMMENDATIONS

Mikkeller
Nelson Sauvignon

Goose Island
Bourbon Country Stout

Three Floyds
Dark Lord Russian
  Imperial Stout

BLACK

The aim was to make a beer that was as extreme as possible – in terms of colour, bitterness and strength – without needing to freeze-distil it. In reality, I just thought it would be fun to see how far I could push it with a beer. All the parameters were ramped up to the max: 18% abv, 500 IBU and 300 EBC. You simply can't make a beer that is more black or more bitter. 'Black' has become very popular, but it is also a beer that divides opinion. Some people think it's the best beer we've made. Others can't stand it. One thing is for certain: it wasn't made for people to enjoy a balanced stout, but to give them an extreme experience. Later on, we developed it further with 'Black Fist', in which we barrel-aged 'Black' ten times in different bourbon barrels, taking the alcohol content up to 26.1% abv.

1000 IBU/
1000 IBU LIGHT

This beer has been made adopting the same extreme approach of 'Black' and is an attempt to make the world's bitterest beer. It completely ignores the theoretical technical limit for a beer of 100 IBU. The general perception in the brewing world is that it is not possible for the human taste palate to register a hop content above 100 IBU and that there is an upper limit for how much alpha acid can be absorbed by a beer. '1000 IBU' is produced using hop extract with a calculated IBU of 1000. By comparison, a regular lager has an IBU of less than 10, while a very hoppy IPA has 100 IBU. Some people drink this beer and say, 'Yuk! It's far too bitter'. But, as with 'Black', the aim was not to make a well-balanced beer but to give people an experience of where the limit for bitterness lies in a beer. '1000 IBU Light' is a version that is lower in alcohol and not quite as sweet.

19

For three years, my most important partner, Proef Brouwerij in Belgium, which brews the majority of Mikkeller's beer, has headed up a PhD project on hops that has incorporated a large number of tastings and brews. Mikkeller has helped with the empirical aspect, and '19' is a result of this. In purely practical terms, we started by brewing 19 different beers using different hop varieties and then held a tasting where people were asked to vote for the beer they thought was best. We then calculated what percentage of participants had voted for the respective hop varieties and added this percentage of each type to a new beer, which we called '19'. The hop variety Simcoe, for example, received 17.14% of the votes, while Amarillo received 14.29%. Other such as Nugget and Williamette received just 0.71%. The content of hops in '19' was thus an intricate composition based on which hop varieties people liked best.

ÅRH HVAD?!

This is my tribute to the Belgian Trappist beer Orval, which in my opinion is the best beer in the world. It has the perfect combination of all that is good in beer – hops, malt and *Brettanomyces* yeast – and you can taste all the elements really clearly. It is both extremely complex and easy to drink. With 'Årh Hvad' I have tried to play on some of the same elements. The Orval

abbey, where the beer is brewed, has an insanely beautiful location surrounded by forest and ruins. It is only open to the public two days a year in September. Pernille and I went there a few years ago but got lost on the way and arrived just too late to spend the night there. Instead, we had to sleep in a house opposite the abbey and make do with visiting the abbey's shop the next day. Ever since, I have wanted to go back to the place, which oozes mysticism and history. And it has to be said it is rather unique to have a much-vaunted brewery run by monks who only produce one commercial beer and yet occupy such a prominent – almost legendary – position on the international beer stage.

CHAPTER 5

SEE, TASTE, SMELL, FEEL

HOW TO TASTE BEER

Drinking a cold lager from the bottle on a hot summer's day can undoubtedly be enjoyable, but if you really want to taste the beer, it should be drunk from a glass. Drinking it from the bottle is like having a cold and a blocked nose – you can't taste anything.

There are a many different types of glasses for beer, and each brewer generally has its own glass bearing its logo. As with wine, the glass is important for allowing you to smell the beer properly and taste all its nuances. Furthermore, there is obviously the aesthetic pleasure of drinking from a nice glass that presents the beer properly and is comfortable to hold. However, choosing the right glass for your beer does not need to be a scientific process.

DRINKING GLASSES

If you stick to four different types of glass, you will have all the bases covered. As a general rule, you should drink lighter, fresher beers, such as lager, weissbier and Berliner Weisse, from tall, solid unstemmed glasses (pint glasses) and heavier, darker beers such as stout and barley wine – plus strong beers such as Belgian tripels and quadrupels – from stemmed glasses.

Well-hopped beers such as IPA and IIPA can be drunk from either a pint glass or a stemmed bowl glass, while higher-alcohol types such as barley wine and imperial stouts should be enjoyed in smaller, modest quantities from small, tulip-shaped stemmed glasses. Spontaneously fermented beers are best in a narrow unstemmed lambic glass.

SMALL STEMMED TULIP GLASS:

BARLEY WINE
IMPERIAL STOUT
BARREL-AGED BEER

PINT GLASS:

LAGER/PILSNER
WEISSBIER
WITBIER
BERLINER WEISSE
BROWN ALE

LARGE STEMMED BOWL GLASS:

IPA
DOUBLE IPA
LIGHT STOUT
PORTER
DUBBEL
TRIPEL
QUADRUPEL

LAMBIC GLASS:

SPONTANEOUSLY
   FERMENTED BEER
WILD ALE
SOUR ALE

You should wash your glasses carefully in warm water, but avoid synthetic detergents as any residues will destroy the head of a beer.

DRINKING<u>TEMPERATURE</u>

The drinking temperature of a beer is of huge importance for how it tastes and smells. A cold temperature inhibits taste nuances, whereas warmth emphasizes them. Obviously, it is a matter of personal taste as to how cold or warm you chose to drink your beer, but when you drink specialty beers it doesn't make sense under any circumstances to kill all the taste notes by serving the beer ice-cold in a glass that has been chilled. A simple rule of thumb is to check the alcohol content and then add two. If the alcohol content of a beer is around 6% abv, then it should be drunk at a temperature of around 8°C (46°F).

TASTE GUIDE

Aroma and taste are inextricably linked, which means that different aromas can also be perceived as taste. Basically, the taste buds can only register five different taste sensations: bitter, sweet, sour, salt and umami. In addition to aroma and taste, however, there are also other aspects that come into play in our experience of beer, especially its appearance and texture.

You should also remember that we all have individual perceptions of aroma and taste, so there is no right or wrong. And the more often you try to describe your taste and aroma sensations, the better you get at it.

Ideally, try the beer together with a snack such as a little cheese, sausage, cured ham or olives. Darker beer is really good with chocolate. Feel free to use this short guide:

1. Pour the beer into your glass so that it forms a good head. Look at it – is it pale or dark, clear or cloudy? Is there a lot of foam?

2. Smell the beer and consider which aromas your nose can detect; sweet, spicy, roasted or fresh?

3. Taste the beer by taking a good gulp and swirling it around your mouth. You do not need to gargle as you would with a mouthwash, but the taste buds will not register the taste properly if you simply sip the beer.

USE YOUR SENSES

YOU SHOULD USE YOUR SIGHT, SMELL, TASTE AND TOUCH WHEN TASTING A BEER.
THE FOLLOWING BUZZ WORDS CAN BE USED AS INSPIRATION FOR THIS PURPOSE.

APPEARANCE
(sense of vision)

COLOUR
HEAD
CLEAR
CLOUDY
SEDIMENT
YEAST RESIDUES

AROMA
(sense of smell)

FRUIT
HOPS
RESIN
NUTS
GRASS
MALT
GRAIN
HERBS
CARAMEL
VANILLA
HONEY
COFFEE
DARK CHOCOLATE

CARDAMOM
NUTMEG
CINAMMON
CLOVES
BLACK PEPPER
SMOKY
BURNT
ROASTED
SPICY
STRONG
BUTTER
SWEETCORN
SULPHUR
BOILED VEGETABLES
YEAST
RANCID
MOULD
PAPER, CARDBOARD
LEATHER
ACID
VINEGAR
ALCOHOL
ROTTEN EGGS
SOLVENT
OAK

SORREL
COCONUT
TEA
HAY
SPIRIT

TASTE
(sense of taste)

BITTER
SWEET
SOUR
SALT
UMAMI

TEXTURE
(sense of touch)

SOFT
RICH
WATERY
CREAMY
WARM
ASTRINGENT
FIZZY
STINGING
STODGY

TASTING SHEET

DATE:	MARKS 1–10:
BREWERY:	NOTES:
NAME:	
BEER TYPE:	
APPEARANCE:	
AROMA:	
TASTE:	
TEXTURE:	
GENERAL IMPRESSION:	

STELLA

Every year, I try to brew a special beer for the Beer Festival. 'Stella' is one such beer that has a very special place in my heart because it is named after my eldest daughter. Originally, I brewed it for the Beer Festival in May 2009, just after she was born, and I have brewed a new edition every year since. So the first edition is called Stella 0 and the latest edition, to date, Stella 5 (for the Beer Festival in May 2014). The beers have been brewed in runs of 150 to 1000, filled into magnum bottles, and all the bottles numbered. I have saved bottle 1 of all the editions of Stella so that my daughter can have them when she grows up. Now I'm the father of another girl, so I'll need to brew a Polly series so that she doesn't feel left out.

AMERICAN DREAM

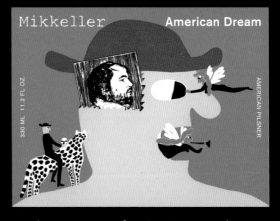

I have a somewhat paradoxical relationship with this beer because, on the one hand, it is our best-selling beer and, on the other hand, it is a lager of 4.6% abv and thus a very long way from what Mikkeller normally stands for, namely extreme, ground-breaking beer. Brewed for the first time in 2009, it was conceived as my version of an American microbrew classic, Sierra Nevada's 'Pale Ale'. It is a highly drinkable beer, but still has lots of hop flavour as if it were a 7% abv IPA.

BLÅ SPØGELSE

Mikkeller has made a number of beers in partnership with the American microbrewery Three Floyds, which I believe to be the coolest brewery in the world. They make well-hopped beers that taste better than everyone else's and have succeeded in creating a unique global image. 'Blå Spøgelse', which translates as 'Blue Ghost', is the latest result of this partnership – a spontaneously fermented beer with loads of blueberries that represents quite a departure from Three Floyds' usual beers. Previously, we had made the 'Goop' series ('goop' being an American term for a sticky, viscous substance), which is a range of barley wines brewed using malts from various cereals, including wheat, oats and rye.

MEXAS RANGER

This beer is a follow-up to Texas Ranger, a porter containing chipotle chili brewed specifically for the Texan market at the request of our American importer. 'Mexas Ranger' has the same basic recipe, but is instead inspired by Mexico. It contains a number of Mexican ingredients, including five different types of chili, tortilla flour, avocado leaves and chocolate. Like most of our labels, the 'Mexas Ranger' label was designed by Mikkeller's art director, Keith Shore, and is a satirical comment on the crazy signs hanging by the roadside at the border crossing from the USA to Mexico that show three Mexicans sprinting across the road with the warnings 'Caution' and 'Prohibido'. On our label, Henry and Sally (Keith Shore's Mikkeller characters) are running back to Mexico with a chili pepper.

CHAPTER 6

BRYG, BREW, BROUW

BREW

YOUR OWN <u>BEER</u>

BEER ESSENTIALLY CONSISTS OF FOUR INGREDIENTS – MALT, HOPS, YEAST AND WATER – AND MAY ALSO BE FLAVOURED WITH VARIOUS SPICES. IT IS ESSENTIAL FOR THE QUALITY OF YOUR BEER THAT YOU CHOOSE YOUR INGREDIENTS WITH CARE AND TRY TO BUY THEM FRESH FROM GOOD SUPPLIERS.

HOPS

The hop plant, *Humulus lupulus*, is a perennial creeper of the hemp family. It only grows wild in Europe and North America, although it is cultivated for beer brewing in many other parts of the world. The biggest producers are Germany, the USA, the Czech Republic and Belgium, while Australia, New Zealand, China and Japan also boast a considerable level of hop production.

For brewing purposes, the mature flowers of the female plant are used. These are called cones because they resemble small fir cones in shape. The hop cones contain a yellowish powdery substance, lupulin, that contains resin. This is what gives hops their bitterness. The lupulin also contains a large number of essential oils, which are vital for the beer's eventual taste and aroma.

In brewing, a distinction is made between bittering hops and aroma hops. Bittering hops are included in the boil from the start with the general aim of imparting bitterness to the beer, while aroma hops are added at the end and give taste and aroma. In some recipes, the same hop variety is used for both purposes. In dry hopping, aroma hops are not used in the boil but are added to the beer during storage. In this way, the hops only add aroma and taste, i.e. no bitterness. You can compare the effect of hops in beer with tea; the longer you leave the hops to infuse, the more bitterness you ultimately obtain.

When brewing, you can either use dried whole-cone hops or hop pellets. The latter consist of dried hop cones that have been crushed and pressed into pellets that resemble rabbit food. Some brewers swear by fully dried hop cones because of their more authentic appearance, but pellets are the preferred product of most microbrewers as they are more practical to handle. They are also more effective because they give a higher yield of the various compounds when the hop is crushed and its leaves and stems discarded. Both forms of dried hop are purchased in vacuum packs, which protect against oxidation.

Hops have been used for brewing since around the 8th century. At the start of the Middle Ages, brewers used extracts of various herbs, such as bog myrtle, juniper and wormwood, to give beer taste, bitterness and storability. Later, from around the 13th to the 17th century, the use of hops spread in Europe, and Denmark began to import hops from, among other places, Germany, where the cultivation of hops can be traced back to the 9th century. The chief reason for the spread of hops was their excellent taste and, not least, their preservative effect. Today, this popular plant's antiseptic quality is not as relevant due to the significantly improved hygiene conditions of modern beer brewing.

Most varieties of hop originally came from Europe and were mainly grown in the southern regions of Germany and Great Britain, where varieties such as Hallertauer Mittelfrüher and Kent Goldings were named after the respective localities from which they came. Chemically speaking, all hop varieties contain the same substances, though in considerably varying concentrations. Modern hop varieties generally have a much higher concentration of alpha acids than traditional varieties because, over time, they have been refined to make them more suitable for brewing.

In terms of taste, it is useful to distinguish between the classic Germanic hop varieties and the American varieties. The former are characterized by earthy, grassy aromas, awhile the more modern American varieties have a higher content of alpha acids and pronounced floral and citrus notes. Generally speaking, the Americans have been more experimental in their hop production, creating a large number of hybrids and triploids from the original European varieties and wild American hops. One of the most popular American hop varieties, Cascade, is a cross between the British Fuggle hop and the Russian Serebrianker hop.

THE BEER'S BITTERNESS: IBU

In the beer world you will often hear mention of the IBU (International Bitterness Units) of a particular beer. Specifically, IBU is a measure of the beer's alpha acids (bitter substances) in milligrams per litre and normally ranges from 1 to 100.

MALT

All beer is based on germinated, dried cereal grains, better known as malt. A large number of cereal varieties can be malted, but barley and wheat are particularly suitable for the purpose because they have a naturally high starch content. The cereal's starch is the platform for the formation of the sugar that eventually turns to alcohol. The cereal cannot be used for brewing before it has been malted (germinated) because it does not naturally contain the enzymes capable of converting the starch to sugar. These enzymes are only formed during the malting process, in which the cereal kernels have to be broken down so that the cereal becomes easier to grind and therefore the starch grains become more accessible.

In the production of malt, the cereal kernels are softened in water, which causes the cereal to germinate. The germination process is interrupted by drying before the kernels sprout at the top, or more precisely when the acrospire has reached 2/3 to 3/4 of the kernel's length. The roasting temperature, water content and interruption point determine the type of malt.

Roasting has a particular influence on the beer's colour and taste. As with coffee beans, the malt becomes darker and stronger in taste the higher the temperature at which it is roasted. Malt can thus be broken down into three different categories. Firstly, pale basic malts, which are lightly roasted, air- or wind-dried and typically extra rich in enzymes. Secondly, kiln-dried malts, which are more thoroughly roasted than basic malts, vary in colour from brown to black and are sometimes bitter with notes of chocolate. Thirdly, caramel malts, which are heated while wet before roasting, promoting sweetness in particular.

Pale malts typically account for the majority of the malt in a beer, while kiln-dried and caramel malts (sometimes known by the generic term 'special malts') are used to supplement colour and taste. For example, a weissbier (wheat beer) is brewed solely with pale malt, while a stout contains lots of kiln-dried malt. The basic malts, however, are essential to the beer because they provide the primary source of starch. Typically, you use 50–75% basic malt for a beer. The remaining percentage may comprise a range of combinations of special malts, other cereals, rice, corn, sugar, etc.

The proteins in beer also come from the malt. The protein content has a major impact on the beer's appearance because it is the protein that produces the head and – in combination with the yeast – can form a more cloudy consistency. Beer types such as witbier and weissbier, for example, are brewed with large amounts of wheat malt, which has a particularly high protein content. It is this that gives these beers their characteristic cloudy look and rich head.

When you buy malt, its colour is defined by an EBC (European Brewing Convention) unit of measurement . The higher the number, the darker the beer colour. You will also come across EBC units in beer recipes, and some breweries include them on their beer labels.

BEER COLOUR: EBC

COLOUR		EBC
	STRAW YELLOW	4-6
	YELLOW	6-10
	GOLDEN	10-12
	AMBER	12-18
	DARK AMBER/LIGHT COPPER	18-28
	COPPER	28-34
	DARK COPPER/LIGHT BROWN	34-38
	BROWN	38-44
	DARK BROWN	44-60
	VERY DARK BROWN	60-70
	BLACK	70-80
	BLACK, OPAQUE	80+

YEAST

It could be said that yeast is the most vital part of beer. Without yeast there would be no alcohol and no carbonic acid. Yeast is a single-celled fungus (myces) that serves the primary function in brewing of converting sugar and carbohydrates from the ground malt into ethanol (alcohol) and CO_2. Later in the brewing process – during secondary fermentation in the bottle – CO_2 is converted to carbonic acid when excess pressure is formed in the sealed bottle. It is this carbonic acid that is released in your beer when you open the bottle. The yeast also forms a large number of important aromatic compounds in the beer, such as fruity or buttery notes. Ultimately, the yeast also determines the level of residual sweetness in the beer because the sweetness depends in part on the favourableness of the conditions under which the yeast has been allowed to ferment. Many breweries are proud to have their own yeast, usually passed down through the generations, and a brewery will often say that the secret to its beer is its yeast.

There are two basic yeast types: bottom-fermenting and top-fermenting. Bottom-fermenting yeast is fermented at low temperatures and collects at the bottom of the fermentation tank, which generally gives a clear beer (for example, lager). All ale types, by contrast, are brewed using top-fermenting yeast, which is fermented at higher temperatures and collects on top of the beer, generally giving the beer a cloudy appearance. The two general yeast types are also known as lager yeast and ale yeast, and within each of the categories there are a wealth of different strains with different characteristics that are used for different beer types.

It is possible to breed yeast strains that have specific properties, such as giving more aroma or creating higher alcohol tolerance. Belgian yeast types, for example, have a very strong aroma, while a lager yeast has a rather neutral aroma because its primary function is to add alcohol and carbonic acid to the beer.

When buying yeast, you can choose between wet or dry yeast. Wet yeast has far more variants, while dry yeast is easier to use, has a longer shelf life and is not as sensitive to temperature fluctuations. Both types should be stored in the refrigerator prior to brewing.

In Denmark, wet yeast from the American producers White Labs and Wyeast is the most common. Yeast from White Labs comes in liquid form in small test tube-like vials made of plastic, while yeast from Wyeast comes in bags that need to be activated a few days before brewing, by squeezing the bag to break a small container inside, thereby allowing the contents of yeast and sugar to mix together.

Brewers often make yeast starters to get the cells to form as efficiently as possible because the number of yeast cells and their vitality are crucial for how quickly a beer begins fermenting. This shortens the most critical period of the process, namely from when the wort is cooled to when the yeast takes over, whilst also avoiding unwanted bacteria. For home-brewing, a vial of wet yeast or a bag of dry yeast should be sufficient, but in some cases you may be unfortunate to come across a 'lazy' yeast, which means the fermentation needs to be kick-started with a yeast starter (more about this later).

WATER

In order to create an optimal brewing process, you need to use water with the right chemical composition and pH. For many brewers, this has a lot to do with traditions and preference – as with bottled mineral water, where people have their personal favourites. Some brewers are obsessed with the taste of the water being just right, while for others it is less important. Traditionally, it was impossible to do anything about the water for brewing, but in modern brewing you can remove substances from the water or add others to get the perfect pH and mineral composition. All breweries have a clearly defined chemical composition for their water that gives an economical and effective brewing water with the right taste.

When you brew at home, it is perfectly fine to use tap water. In general, water can be used if it tastes and smells neutral. In countries where there is a lot of nitrate or chlorine in the water, however, an unpleasant off-flavour can easily arise, which means you should resort to mineral water.

SPICES

Like hops, spices can be added at different stages of the brewing process: they may simmer in the mix throughout the boiling stage, or they may be added at the end or during storage. Regardless, their chief purpose is to lend taste and aroma to the beer.

Generally speaking, spices have a very powerful effect on the flavour of beer, so it is important to add them in very small quantities in relation to the other ingredients such as hops. Beer has traditionally always been flavoured with spices such as bog myrtle and juniper, which were also used as preservatives before hops came into use.

Among the most common beer spices are orange peel and coriander, which give witbier and other ales their characteristic fresh taste, but today microbrewers all over the world tend to be highly adventurous when it comes to giving beer a spicy character. In principle, it is only the imagination that imposes any limits. At the more extreme end of the spectrum, the Evil Twin brewery has put Spanish cured Iberico ham in its 'Biscotti Break Special Edition', while the American brewer Dogfish Head has added real moon dust from a meteorite to its Celest-Jewel-Ale. At Mikkeller, over the years we have used everything in our beers, from vanilla to weasel coffee (passed through the digestive system of a weasel), pepper, truffles, passion fruit, aniseed, cinnamon and smoked chipotle chili.

EQUIPMENT

EQUIPMENT

The following tools are an excellent investment if you are planning to brew on a regular basis. Fortunately, brewing equipment is relatively cheap compared to a lot of other hobby equipment, and if need be you can get by with less. For example, the various suppliers of brewing equipment offer a beginner's set for around £85-95 (US$140-155). If you are bitten by the homebrew bug, however, it is certainly advisable to invest in more advanced equipment, which will make the brewing process considerably easier.

These guidelines are based on brewing in an electric boiler with a tap, which enables you to brew wherever you wish – in the kitchen, the shed or outdoors – provided you have access to clean water and electricity. Alternatively, you can replace the electric boiler with a large stock pot (30 litres/8 gallons) and brew on an induction or gas cooker. If, as recommended here, you decide to use a plastic mash tun, it is advisable to pack it in matting or a similar material so that it retains the heat better during mashing.

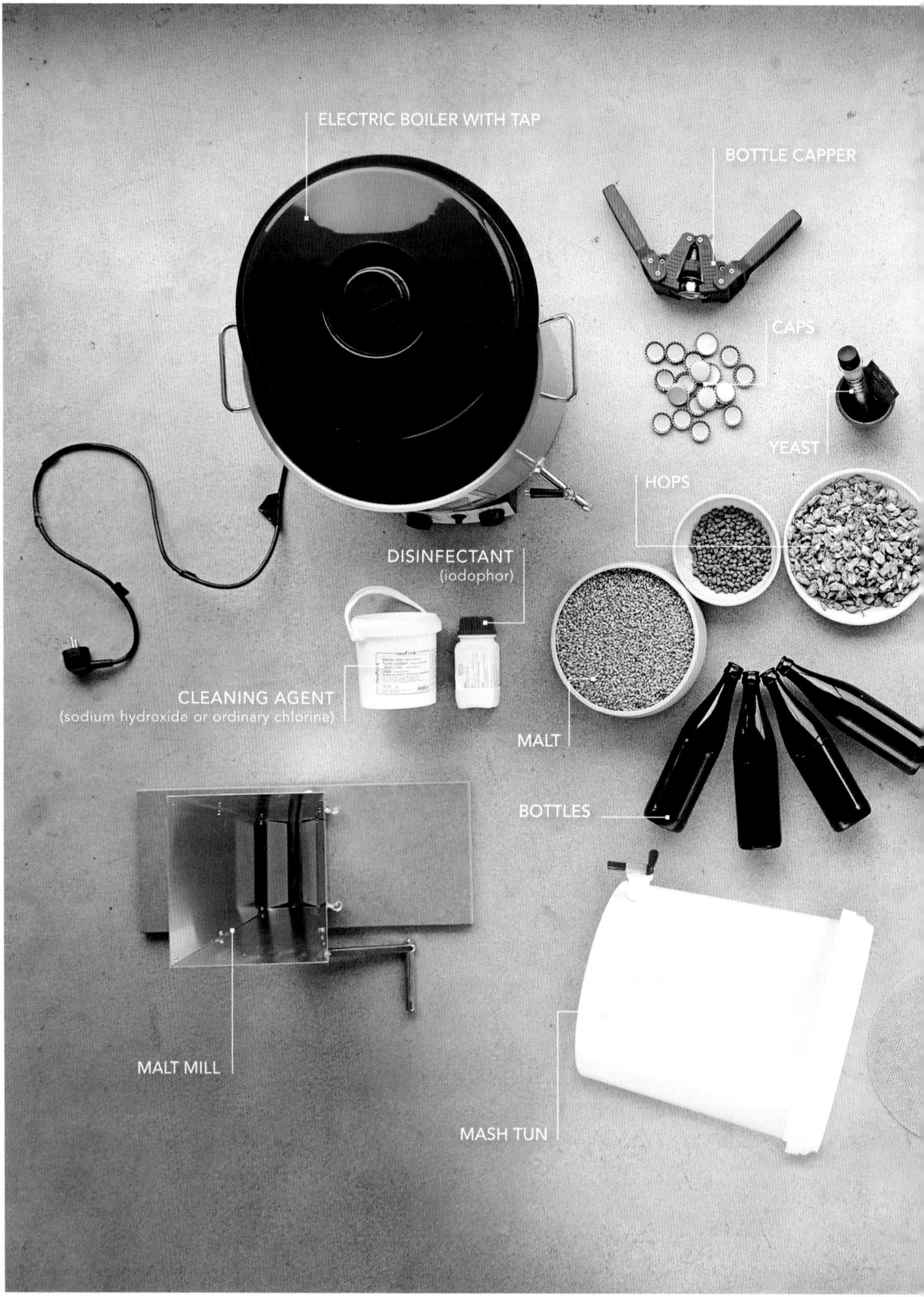

ELECTRIC BOILER WITH TAP

BOTTLE CAPPER

CAPS

YEAST

HOPS

DISINFECTANT
(iodophor)

CLEANING AGENT
(sodium hydroxide or ordinary chlorine)

MALT

BOTTLES

MALT MILL

MASH TUN

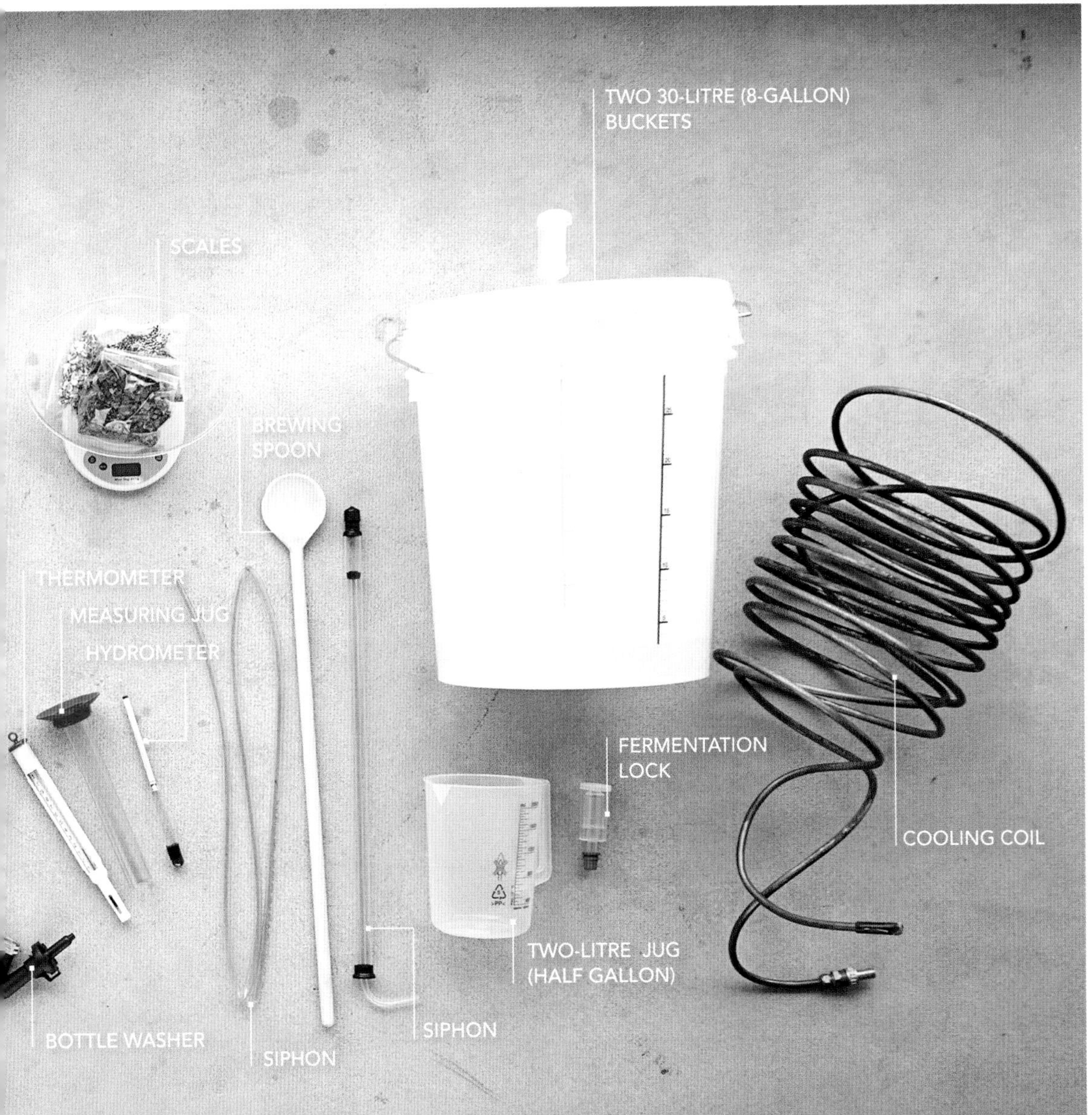

TWO 30-LITRE (8-GALLON) BUCKETS
SCALES
BREWING SPOON
THERMOMETER
MEASURING JUG
HYDROMETER
FERMENTATION LOCK
COOLING COIL
TWO-LITRE JUG (HALF GALLON)
BOTTLE WASHER
SIPHON
SIPHON

WHERE TO BUY YOUR EQUIPMENT

The following online stores sell all the ingredients, tools, cleaning agents and bottles you will need for your brewing.

ART OF BREWING: www.art-of-brewing.co.uk

BREWSTORE: www.brewstore.co.uk

HOMEBREW SHOP: www. thehome-brew-shop.co.uk

BEER AT HOME: www.beerathome.com

HOMEBREW STUFF : www.homebrewstuff.com

MORE BEER: www.morebeer.com

AUSSIE BREWER: www.aussiebrewer.com.au

ONLY ONE RIGHT WAY:

ALL GRAIN

When you start brewing, you realistically have three options: kit, semi-grain or all-grain. Brewing with a kit was common in the 1970s, when it became a popular hobby to go into a pharmacy store and buy a DIY brewing kit, which simply comprised a bottle of malt syrup with hop flavouring and a packet of dried yeast. You poured the syrup into a demijohn or a bathtub, scooped in hot water, then added yeast, and a week later you had a beer – or at least a malted alcoholic beverage. It goes without saying the taste was not great.

In the case of semi-grain brewing, also called extract brewing, you use different forms of malt syrup or spray malt (malt in powdered form). You can also add small amounts of whole grain malt to give the brew flavour and colour. The result can be okay, but in terms of quality it is impossible to concoct anything that is on a par with the beer produced in professional microbreweries.

This means that all-grain brewing is the only one right way to start brewing at home. It is a far more elaborate process than the others, but produces results that compare favourably with your favourite pale ale or stout. In some cases all-grain home-brewing can be even better, because it is far easier to adjust and correct 20 litres (5 gallons) of home-brew than 2000 litres (530 gallons) of beer in a brewery.

Having said that, the process still requires a good deal of patience, practice and care, and you should set aside the best part of a day for each brew: an all-grain brew takes around eight hours, so it's a matter of following all the steps in the process very carefully. Once you get an infection in the beer, you risk having to discard a whole day's work.

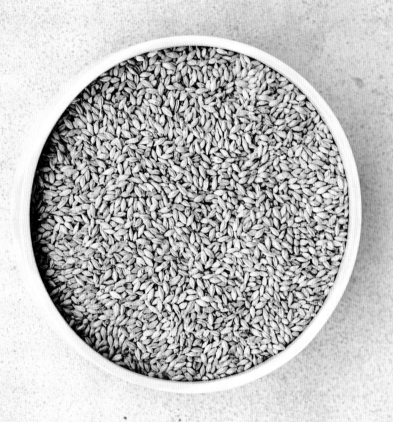

Whenever I'm asked how you become a good brewer, I answer 'cleaning, cleaning, cleaning'! I can't stress enough how important it is to think hygienically throughout the brewing process. Scimping on cleaning is probably the classic home-brewer's error and often results in infected beer. Professional brewers spend as much time on cleaning as on the beer itself, so from the very beginning you should be prepared to make cleaning a major part of the process. You need to thoroughly clean and disinfect pots, buckets, brewing spoons and other tools before you begin, and it's equally important to do so as you go along also. And remember to keep your hands clean!

Choose your cleaning agents with care because perfumed products can impart unwanted flavour to the beer. Brewing stores sell cleaning agents specifically designed for brewing, but you can go a very long way with a bottle of chlorine from the supermarket. When I was brewing at home, I always cleaned with chlorine, then rinsed my buckets and pots thoroughly in cold water (but be aware that you can't use chlorine for metal tools). I also made up a solution of water and iodophor in my fermenting bucket and left all my tools soaking until I was ready to use them. This meant the bucket was disinfected when I came to use it and I always had clean tools handy.

> Choose your cleaning agents with care because perfumed products may impart unwanted flavour into the beer.

ALL GRAIN

– STEP BY STEP

Generally speaking, you can divide the all-grain brewing process into two parts: wort production and fermentation. The wort is the mix of water, malt, hops and spices that is made before you add yeast. A traditional brewery has two sections – a brewhouse for the wort and a fermentation cellar for fermentation and storage. As a rule, it takes around eight hours to brew a beer, two to three weeks to ferment and store it, and one week to secondary ferment the bottle. In the case of an ale, you should therefore count on around four weeks from when you brew the beer until when you can open the bottle. In the case of a lager, it takes around twice as long to ferment and store it.

TERMS USED IN THE BREWING PROCESS

MASH:
The actual mix of water and malt.

MASHING-IN:
The process of mixing the water and malt.

MASHING:
The steeping of the malt in hot water (roughly 64-70°C/147-158°F) for 1-1.5 hours.

MASH SOLIDS:
The solid part of the mash.

WORT:
The liquid part of the mash prior to the addition of yeast.

MASHING-OUT:
The recirculation of the wort through the malt's natural filter to make it clear.

SPARGING:
The pouring of hot water (around 78°C/172°F) over the malt to extract the final sugar after mashing-out.

BITTERING HOPS:
Added at the start of the boiling process, mainly to impart bitterness to the beer and provide a preservative effect.

AROMA HOPS:
Added at the end of the brewing process, mainly to add aroma and taste as well as provide a preservative effect.

DRY-HOPPING:
The addition of hops immediately prior to or during storage.

1 PREPARATION

Before brewing for the first time, it is important that you carefully read through the brewing instructions and recipe. Familiarize yourself with your equipment and your ingredients beforehand. For example, how do you use and read your hydrometer? Check that you have all the tools you will need – including any spare parts – and ensure they are cleaned in advance. When you begin brewing, you will need to be constantly alert and you will not have time to waste on a cooling coil that doesn't have the right thread for the tap or a bucket that isn't completely clean.

All the same, you should not expect the entire process to go smoothly from the word go, even if you are well prepared. A large part of the brewing craft can only be mastered by gaining your own experiences through repeated brewing, so don't lose heart if something goes wrong. And most importantly of all, be patient!

2 | **MALT** GRIDING

● The very first thing you need to do is to grind your malt. It's important to adjust your grind correctly. The malt should not be ground too fine or too coarse. As a rule of thumb, the grains should be chopped into three to five pieces.

❞ MIKKEL'S NOTES

Grinding allows release of the malt's enzymes and starch grains so that during brewing the enzymes can convert the starch to fermentable sugar molecules (i.e. make them available to the yeast), but it also makes the malt more vulnerable. It is therefore best to grind the malt you need for a specific brew immediately in advance of the brewing day or on the day itself.

If you buy ground malt, buy it for one brew at a time so it is not lying around for a long time. Whole or unground malt can be safely stored in a silo for years, whereas ground malt quickly loses its flavour and becomes susceptible to fungus and mould.

3 | MASHING-IN

- Fill the electric pot with water and heat it up to the stated mashing temperature plus 6–7°C (43-45°F). This temperature is called the strike temperature.

🗩🗩 MIKKEL'S NOTES

The strike temperature is higher than the mashing temperature because both the equipment and the malt are roughly at room temperature upon mixing (if you brew indoors, that is) and the temperature of the mash solids generally therefore falls.

- The malt and water now need to be mixed in your mash tun. Start by pouring 2 litres (half gallon) of water per kilo (2.2lbs) of malt into the mash tun, then add the malt slowly while stirring thoroughly. It is important to stir the malt properly so there are no dry lumps left in the mash solids. Add more water until you have around 2.5-3 litres (half to three quarters galllon) of water per kilo (2.2.lbs) of malt and the mix has a semi-solid consistency that can still be stirred – roughly like a ryebread dough.

- While you are mashing, you should refill your electric boiler and heat the water to 78°C (173°F) so it is ready for sparging.

- During the actual mashing, when you allow the malt to infuse in the water for 1-1.5 hours at the stated mashing temperature (check the precise mashing time and temperature in the recipe), you should regularly stir the mash and ensure that the temperature is constant. Add a little cold water if it gets too high and a little boiling water if it gets too low.

🔻🔻 MIKKEL'S NOTES

In this process, the natural enzymes in the malt are released and convert starch to sugar.

The sugar content of the wort is absolutely essential for the final result as it is the sugar that is converted to alcohol during fermentation. A few beer styles require you to vary the mashing temperature during the process, but the simplest practical advice is to mash at the same temperature throughout.

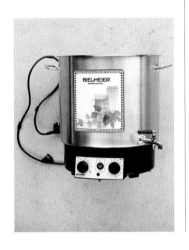

The mashing temperature should be 64–70°C/147–158°F (precisely stated in the recipe) as this temperature range gives the enzymes in the malt the optimum working conditions. At a high temperature, you are moving towards a beer with more body and fullness, whereas a low temperature gives a cleaner, simpler beer. At an excessively low mashing temperature, the enzymes become lazy, whereas too high a temperature makes them inactive. It is obviously therefore important to regularly check the temperature with your thermometer during mashing.

4 | MASHING-<u>OUT</u>

- You now need to draw off your wort through the tap at the bottom of the mash tun. The first wort you draw off should be poured straight back into the mash. Use both one-litre (quarter gallon) jugs so that you can replace one with the other as you pour in the wort. Be careful not to go too quickly: the wort should flow slowly from the tap at around 0.5 litres (one tenth gallon) per minute. Once you have opened the tap, you should not close it again; there should be a constant flow.

,, MIKKEL'S NOTES

This process is called recirculation. During recirculation, the husks from the malt settle in the bottom of the
mash tun and form a natural filter that sifts impurities
from the wort. As a rule of thumb, the sediment is acting
as a sieve when the drawn-off liquid no longer contains
visible malt particles.

- Now you can start drawing off the wort into your 30-litre (8-gallon) bucket. At the same time, you should start sparging. Gently pour the 78°C (173°F) water from your electric boiler over the mash as you slowly draw off the wort into your bucket. It is important to ensure that the mash solids are always covered with a small layer of liquid. The purpose of sparging is to extract all the sugar from the malt. Continue this process until you have 25 litres (6.6 gallons) of preboil wort in your bucket.

- Check the sugar content of your wort by taking a sample and cooling it to 20°C/68°F (for example, in a clean, empty tin can standing in cold water in the sink). Pour the cooled wort into your measuring jug and measure the boil gravity (BG) with your hydrometer. If you have accurately followed the recipe, the sugar content of your wort should now correspond to the BG stated in the recipe.

If your BG is not as expected, you need to make a few adjustments earlier in the process the next time you brew.

The recipes in this book have been produced based on a mashing efficiency of 75%, which means using 75% of the sugar content of the malt. If your BG is too low, this means your efficiency has also been too low. You can increase it by grinding the malt slightly finer next time.

If, however, your BG is too high, you can try cutting back slightly on the amount of malt in the next brew.

Finally, a BG that is too low may be due to poor extraction of the sugar during sparging, so take care with this part of the process.

BG

5

BOILING AND ADDITION OF HOPS

- You now need to pour the wort into your empty electric boiler and begin heating it. While the wort is heating up to boiling point, weigh out your bittering hops.

- If your BG was too low, you can boil the wort for a short time and measure again until it has the desired BG. If your BG was too high, you can add water to reduce the desired sugar content. Only when you have the right BG should you add your first hops and begin timing as per the recipe.

- When the beer boils, it quickly foams, so be careful that it does not boil over and always have a bottle of cold water beside your boiling tun that you can pour in if it begins to foam too much.

⁇ MIKKEL'S NOTES

The purpose of the boiling process is to sterilize the wort, extract bitterness, aroma and taste from the hops, and precipitate proteins, etc., in the wort to make it clearer.

The longer you boil, the more concentrated your wort becomes. Prolonged boiling has the effect of cara-melizing the sugar, which gives the beer less fermentability (i.e. reduces its ability to ferment). This is a benefit if, for example, you want a very thick, black beer - an imperial stout for example. Prolonged boiling thus gives a stronger, richer beer, but less volume overall.

- As soon as the wort boils, you should add your bittering hops. The time is given in the recipe as, for example, 60 min (1 hour before the end of boiling) or 1 min (1 min before the end of boiling). As soon as you have added your bittering hops, you should weigh out your aroma hops so they are ready to be added later in the boiling process. Also, take your yeast out of the refrigerator so that it can warm to room temperature prior to use.

- While the wort is boiling, it is a good idea to spend some time cleaning; for example, you can disinfect the fermenting bucket and the fermentation lock. It is also a good idea to draw off 2–3 litres (half to three quarters gallon) of the boiling wort through the tap into your measuring jug in order to disinfect the tap before drawing off the cooled wort into the fermenting bucket. Do this as close as possible to the end of boiling. Pour the wort back into the boiler and finish by putting tin foil on the tap to keep it clean prior to drawing off.

- It is now time to add your aroma hops and any spices. The aroma hops are generally added during the final part of boiling – from 1 to around 15 min before your wort has finished boiling. It is a good idea to boil the cleaned cooler with the wort for the final 5-10 min of boiling in order to disinfect it before use in cooling.

Once you have mastered the basic elements of the brewing process, you can experiment with spices. But use your common sense. For example, you don't boil your coffee, so it isn't smart to boil coffee in your beer. You also wouldn't boil fresh spices for a long time in your soup, so it makes sense to add them when the boiling has finished.

6 OXIDATION, COOLING AND FERMENTATION

● When the wort has finished boiling, you need to cool it to fermentation temperature (stated in the recipe). Rapid cooling is important to minimize the time for which the wort is vulnerable to infection. You should therefore use your cooling coil. It is beneficial to stir the wort regularly during cooling in order to speed up the process, but be aware of hygiene.

● Once the wort has cooled, it needs to be transferred to the fermenting bucket. Start by drawing off 0.5 litres (1 pint), then discard it so that the tap has been washed. Then transfer a little wort to your measuring jug and measure the original gravity (OG). Note down the result – you will need to use it later to calculate your alcohol content. Then let your wort splash from the tap into the fermenting bucket.

❞❞ MIKKEL'S NOTES

This is the only point in the brewing process where oxygen is desired. Oxidation is important for allowing the yeast to propagate. When the oxidation gives out after a few hours, the yeast begins to convert the sugar to alcohol and the CO_2 and does not therefore propagate as quickly.

● Now add your yeast. Make sure you thoroughly mix it into the wort with your disinfected spoon. Fit the fermentation lock in the hole in the lid. This ensures that no impurities get into the wort and also relieves some of the pressure when the yeast begins to form CO_2. When fermentation begins – which should be within a few hours and no more than 24 hours – your fermentation lock will begin to bubble. Now all you can do is wait. Fortunately, the vast majority of beers will ferment at room temperature temperature (20–22°C/68-72°F). A few types, however, ferment at 10°C (50 °F), while a saison, for example, ferments at 30°C (86°F) or higher.

For small brews of less than 25 litres (6 gallons), a yeast starter should not be necessary. If for one reason or another, however, your yeast is still sluggish (maybe it has passed its expiry date or not been stored at a cold-enough temperature), it may be necessary to use a yeast starter to boost the yeast.

A simple way of making a yeast starter is to put 1 litre (2 pints) of pasteurized apple juice into a freezer bag, add a sachet of yeast and tie the bag closed. The sugar in the apple juice begins to ferment and the CO_2 is able to escape because the bag is not sealed.

Remember to keep the bag clean and protected from sources of infection. After 2-3 days, add all the juice to your wort as one large portion of wet yeast.

YEAST STARTER

7 STORAGE AND BOTTLING

● Your beer has finished fermenting when no more bubbles are emitted through the fermentation lock or there is a very long interval between them. You can check whether fermentation is complete by measuring the final gravity (FG) at an interval of a few days. If it remains unchanged, the conversion of sugar to alcohol is complete. If it has fallen, you should leave the beer to ferment for a few more days. You can now calculate the alcohol content by subtracting FG from OG and dividing by 7.5.

$$\frac{\text{original gravity - final gravity}}{7.5}$$

● It is now time to rack your beer. Here, you should use the siphon to transfer the beer from one fermentation bucket to a second disinfected bucket. During fermentation, the dead yeast cells have sunk to the bottom and you should make sure that you transfer as few of them as possible when racking.

● Now the beer can be stored. During storage in the second fermentation bucket, even more of the yeast will settle and make your beer clearer. If you store the beer in a refrigerator (but above freezing temperature), the process will speed up. As a rule, the beer should be stored for 1-2 weeks.

● If your beer is to be dry-hopped, it can be beneficial to do this at room temperature as this will draw more aroma out of the hops than in a cooled beer. Some brewers prefer to use a hop sock, but adding the hops directly to the beer gives a far greater yield. It just takes a little longer because you need to re-rack your beer after about one week to sift out the hops. Proceed by trial and error. How the hops precipitate and how long it takes will depend on temperature and whether you use pellets or whole hop cones.

● Before bottling, you should disinfect your bottles using an iodophor solution and then wash them thoroughly using a bottle washer.

♥♥ MIKKEL'S NOTES

● When bottling, you should start by dissolving a quantity of sugar (see table) in some boiling water, adding it to the beer in the storage tank and stirring thoroughly to distribute the sugar solution. The added sugar will kick-start the fermentation in the bottle, which will generate a small amount of alcohol, but even more importantly CO_2.

grams (oz) of sugar per litre (34fl oz) of beer

	Beer 5°C (41°F)	Beer 10°C (50°F)	Beer 15°C (59°F)	Beer 20°C (68°F)
Ale (non-wheat)	0.2–2.2	1.2–3.2	1.9–3.9	2.5–4.5
Lager	3.0–5.0	4.0–6.0	4.7–6.7	5.3–7.3
Wheat beer	7.4–12.2	8.4–13.2	9.1–13.9	9.7–14.5

● Now you need to once again use the disinfected siphon to transfer the beer from the bucket into the bottles, after which they can be capped. As the CO_2 cannot escape from the sealed bottles, it will be dissolved in the beer as carbonic acid. Secondary fermentation in the bottle also serves the function of extending the beer's shelf life. The fermentation will generally take one week at room temperature. If no carbonic acid has formed in your beer after one week, try storing the bottles at a slightly warmer temperature. If, by contrast, the beer is bubbling, it is ready to be refrigerated.

BARREL-AGED BEER

You also have the option of putting your beer in barrels, but it is a lot more expensive than using bottles and also more tricky to handle.

Barrelling also requires that, in addition to the actual barrels, you procure a CO_2 canister and a cooler.

For this reason, this book only discusses bottling.

WHAT I <u>AM</u> DOING WRONG IF…

My beer smells sour, rotten, sulphury, vegetable-like, stings in the mouth, is astringent (feels like it's drying out your mouth) or similar?

Unfortunately, your beer is probably infected. It is very rare that infected beer is harmful to drink, but the taste can be horrible. Consider reviewing your cleaning routines and methods. This can give you a clue as to where things may be going wrong in the brewing process.

My fermentation bucket is not emitting any gas or the beer is no longer fermenting but is still very sweet?

Your yeast has probably not had good enough conditions in which to work. First, try reviving it by gently shaking the tank. If this doesn't work, inject a little air into the beer by blowing through a hose or using an aquarium pump. The cause of the problem may be too little yeast nutrition, too little oxygen in the wort, too little added yeast or non-conformant temperatures (whether too high or too low). If none of these prove to be the cause, you need to use a yeast starter.

My beer is very cloudy and appears muddy

This may be due to a bacterial infection, although in that case you should also be able to taste it. If this is not the case, it is more likely to be a problem that has arisen during mashing and sparging. Next time, try recirculating the wort more thoroughly to achieve a clearer wort. Also consider whether you need to boil the wort for longer. If necessary, add clarifying products such as Protafloc or Irish Moss. These products bind to the impurities in the wort during boiling and are precipitated perfectly naturally.

My beer has very little taste and I am not achieving the stated alcohol content?

You may have been a bit too quick with the sparging. This should take up to two hours. Possibly the sparging water was able to run down the sides and did not come into proper contact with the mash. You can also consider whether your malt composition is good enough – whether, for example, the malt has been ground finely enough? Did you stir thoroughly enough during mashing? Did the mash stand for long enough at the right temperature to convert all the starch to sugar?

My beer smells of boiled vegetables or sweetcorn

You have probably got a lot of DMS (dimethyl sulphide) in your beer. This is produced in the hot wort but can be evaporated off at the same time. It is important that the wort is boiled without a lid so that condensation cannot drip back into the wort. And ideally it should boil powerfully. Furthermore, it is important to cool the wort as quickly as possible once boiling is complete.

My sparging has almost stopped or the liquid is running very slowly

This may be due to impurities in the wort. If you have the opportunity to clean the tap or other equipment of fouling, you should do so. Otherwise, try heating the mash slightly – ideally to 72-75°C (161-167°F) – or use slightly hotter sparging water (maximum 80°C/176°F). The cause of the problem could be poorly or too finely ground malt. If you are brewing with large amounts of rye, oats or wheat, which have a lot of soluble fibre and therefore give a slow sparging, you need to be patient. Sparging can take up to two hours, though it should not take any longer.

My beer tastes slightly sickly – of butter or caramel

It may be that the maturing process has not removed the by-product diacetyl. If possible, try letting the beer mature for longer in the yeast bucket, ideally at 14-20°C (57-68°F). If the beer is already in the bottle, patience could resolve the problem. Otherwise, you could try adding more yeast and waiting longer. If you are making a lager, try raising the temperature during storage to around 15-17°C (59-62°F) for a few days to let the diacetyl evaporate off. This is called a diacetyl rest. Certain bacterial infections can also cause high amounts of diacetyl.

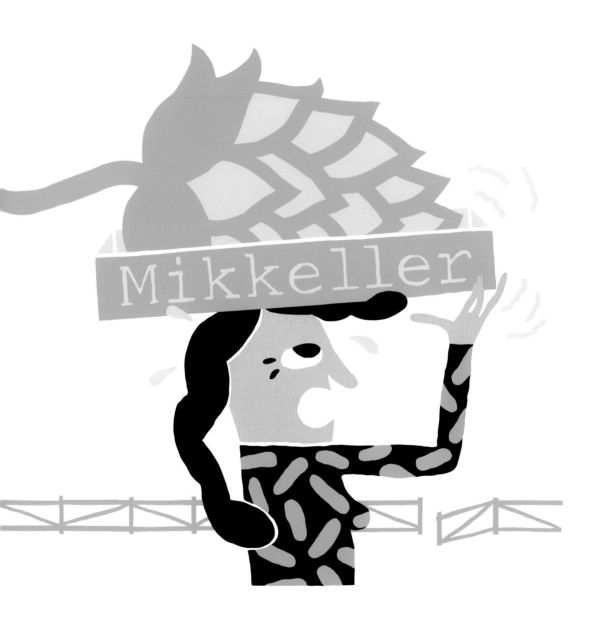

1. CLONING A BEER

FOR THE NOVICE ...

When I began home-brewing, without a doubt the thing that taught me most was trying to copy a beer that I really liked. Most beginners are likely to set about brewing a lot of different beer types from the start. My advice is: find your favourite beer type and try to clone it. If it's an IPA, start by brewing your own IPA and then compare it with your favourite by tasting them at the same time and reviewing which parameters need to be adjusted in order for your beer to taste like your model beer. If, for example, your IPA is paler, you need to add darker malt types. If it is sweeter, you could try reducing the mashing temperature or cutting back on the amount of sweet caramel malts. You could also try adding more bittering hops to balance out the sweetness better.

This is a process that requires lots of patience, and you should be prepared for a good deal of trial and error before you finally succeed. On the other hand, you will acquire a range of invaluable tools and a solid basic understanding of the brewing processes that will benefit you greatly as you progress in your brewing. Quite simply, you will end up with better beers because you will become a more experienced and, hence, more skilful brewer.

2. GETTING T̲O̲ KNOW YOUR INGREDIE̲NTS

FOR BREWERS WITH SOME EXPERIENCE ...

A recipe will always include several different hop and malt types, so for your own recipes you can choose from a wealth of different yeast types. There is a huge benefit in getting to know the various hop, malt and yeast types and finding out what effects they have when you isolate them from the other ingredients. For example, you learn more about hops by dividing a wort into several portions then boiling and dry-hopping them separately with different hop types – Amarillo in one portion, Cascade in another, etc. This will give you a basic appreciation of how the different hop types smell and taste. Repeat the trial with yeast by brewing 25 litres (6.6 gallons) of wort and dividing it into five different 5-litre (1.3-gallon) buckets, then adding five different yeast types. You can try the same with malt, but it is a slightly more complicated project as it requires you to make a brew for each malt type you want to test.

3. MAKING A STRONG BEER

FOR EXPERIENCED BREWERS ...

O nce you feel you are on relatively solid ground and have gained some experience of the brewing process, you can try making a really strong beer. See how high you can get the alcohol content by experimenting with yeast types, mashing temperatures, oxidation, sugar addition and perhaps added enzymes. This will give you a thorough understanding of the function of the different ingredients and of the chemical processes of brewing.

MORE INFORMATION ON BREWING AND BREWING PROCESSES

BASIC BOOKS

RAY DANIELS
Designing Great Beers

DAVE MILLER
The Complete Handbook of Home Brewing

JOHN PALMER
How to Brew

CHARLIE PAPAZIAN
The New Complete Joy of Home Brewing

GRAHAM WHEELER
CAMRA's Complete Home Brewing

Additionally, the website Brewersfriend.com has brought together a mass of information for the beginner, including the BeerCalc tool for putting together your own recipes, or modifying or adjusting an existing recipe.

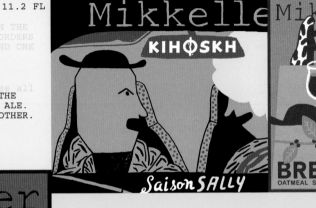

 GOOD BEGINNERS' RECIPES

 LEVEL OF DIFFICULTY

 LEVEL OF DIFFICULTY

 LEVEL OF DIFFICULTY

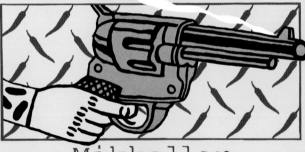

Mikkeller
TEXAS RANGER
BREWED WITH SPICES, ALMOND MILK, COCOA, CHILIES, BLACK BEANS & AVOCADO LEAVES

CROSSING THE BORDER

Mikkeller

Mikkeller
斯特拉四

IMPERIAL MILK STOUT
AGED IN GRAND MARNIER BARRELS

STELLA 4

Mikkeller
RAUCHPILS

Mikkelle

1.4%
ALC/VOL

330 ml

CHAPTER 7

BEER RECIPES

IT'S ALIVE!

BELGIAN WILD ALE

GREEN GOLD

AMERICAN-STYLE INDIA PALE ALE

Mikkeller

SALLY THROWS HER PURSE ON THE
STOOL BESIDE HER. HENRY ORDERS
SALLY ANOTHER PALE ALE AND ONE
FOR HIMSELF

<u>ACT ONE</u>

<u>INT. Mikkeller - NIGHT</u>

HENRY & SALLY ARRIVE AT THE
BAR. SALLY ORDERS A PALE ALE.
SHE TAKES A SIP. THEN ANOTHER.

SALLY
We should drink these all   *
night.

HENRY
(Nods in agreement)   *

HENRY

How is it?   *

SALLY

SALLY
I'm in loveee.   *

All other pales pale.   *

ALL OTHER PALE ALES

STYLE: AMERICAN PALE ALE

STATISTICS

Volume	20 litres (5⅓ gallons)
Boil volume	25 litres (6½ gallons)
OG	1058
BG	1046
FG	1012
Alcohol	6.0% abv
Colour	19 EBC
Bitterness	~55 IBU

HOPS

Simcoe	13.0% alpha	25g (1oz)	60 min
Centennial	8.8% alpha	15g (½oz)	10 min
Santiam	11.9% alpha	10g (⅓oz)	1 min
Nugget	12.8% alpha	15g (½oz)	1 min
Simcoe	13.0% alpha	15g (½oz)	dry hop
Nugget	12.8% alpha	15g (½oz)	dry hop
Warrior	12.0% alpha	15g (½oz)	dry hop
Amarillo	9.5% alpha	15g (½oz)	dry hop

MASHING

Pale Malt	6 EBC	2800g (6lb 3oz)
Munich I Malt	22 EBC	800g (1lb 12oz)
Cara Amber Malt	70 EBC	475g (1lb 1oz)
Cara Pils Malt	4 EBC	325g (11½oz)
Cara Pils Malt	4 EBC	625g (1lb 6oz)

Total malt	5025g (11lbs)
Mashing programme	65°C (149°F for 60 min)

FERMENTATION

Yeast	1056 American Ale
Temperature	19-21°C (66-70°F)

Mikkeller

BEER GEEK

BREAKFAST

OATMEAL STOUT BREWED WITH COFFEE

BEER GEEK BREAKFAST

STYLE: OATMEAL STOUT WITH COFFEE

STATISTICS

Volume	20 litres (5⅓ gallons)
Boil volume	25 litres (6½ gallons)
OG	1074
BG	1059
FG	1017
Alcohol	7.5% abv
Colour	106 EBC
Bitterness	~100+ IBU

MASHING

Pilsner Malt	3 EBC	3300g (7lb 4oz)
Flaked Mats	5 EBC	1650g (3lb 10oz)
Cara Amber I Malt	90 EBC	365g (12½oz)
Brown Malt	150 EBC	365g (12½oz)
Pale Chocolate Malt	500 EBC	365g (12½oz)
Chocolate Malt	940 EBC	180g (6⅓oz)
Roasted Barley	1150 EBC	365g (12½oz)
Smoked Malt	6 EBC	180g (6⅓oz)

Total malt	6770g (14lbs 14oz)
Mashing programme	67°C (152°F) for 60 min

HOPS

Centennial	10.0% alpha	50g (1¾oz)	60 min
Cascade	5.7% alpha	20g (¾oz)	60 min
Cascade	5.7% alpha	45g (1½oz)	15 min
Centennial	10.0% alpha	45g (1½oz)	5 min
Cascade	5.7% alpha	10g (¼oz)	5 min

FERMENTATION

Yeast	1056 American Ale
Temperature	21-23°C (70-73°F)

COMMENTS

0.5 litres (1 pint) ground coffee made with 50g (1¾oz) coffee added a few days before bottling.

BEER GEEK BACON

STYLE: SMOKED STOUT WITH COFFEE

STATISTICS

Volume	20 litres (5⅓ gallons)
Boil volume	25 litres (6½ gallons)
OG	1074
BG	1059
FG	1017
Alcohol	7.5% abv
Colour	106 EBC
Bitterness	~100+ IBU

MASHING

Smoked Malt	6 EBC	3480g (7lb 11oz)	
Flaked Mats	5 EBC	1650 (3lb 10oz)	
Cara Munich I Malt	90 EBC	365g (12½oz)	
Brown Malt	150 EBC	365g (12½oz)	
Pale Chocolate Malt	500 EBC	365g (12½oz)	
Chocolate Malt	940 EBC	180g (6⅓oz)	
Roasted Barley	1150 EBC	365g (12½oz)	

Total malt	6770g (14lbs 14oz)
Mashing programme	67°C (152°F) for 60 min

HOPS

Centennial	10.0% alpha	50g (1¾oz)	60 min
Cascade	5.7% alpha	20g (¾oz)	60 min
Cascade	5.7% alpha	45g (1½oz)	15 min
Centennial	10.0% alpha	45g (1½oz)	5 min
Cascade	5.7% alpha	10g (¼oz)	5 min

FERMENTATION

Yeast	1056 American Ale
Temperature	21-23°C (70-73°F)

COMMENTS

0.5 litres (1 pint) ground coffee made with 50g (1¾oz) coffee added a few days before bottling.

RAUCHPILS

STYLE: SMOKED BEER

STATISTICS

Volume	20 litres (5⅓ gallons)
Boil volume	25 litres (6½ gallons)
OG	1045
BG	1036
FG	1010
Alcohol	4.6% abv
Colour	11 EBC
Bitterness	~26 IBU

MASHING

Pilsner Malt	4 EBC	1350g	(2lb 15½oz)
Munich I Malt	23 EBC	600g	(1lb 5oz)
Cara Pils Malt	5 EBC	600g	(1lb 5oz)
Smoked Malt	6 EBC	1350g	(2lb 15½oz)

Total malt	3900g (8lbs 9½oz)
Mashing programme	65°C (149°F) for 60 min

HOPS

Hallertauer	6.6% alpha	18g (½oz)	60 min
Tettnanger	3.8% alpha	18g (½oz)	10 min
Hallertauer	6.6% alpha	12g (⅓oz)	5 min
Tettnanger	3.8% alpha	12g (⅓oz)	5 min
Tettnanger	3.8% alpha	25g (1oz)	dry hop

FERMENTATION

Yeast	WLP820 Octoberfest/Märzen Lager
Temperature	11-12°C (52-53.5°F)

STATESIDE IPA Mikkeller

STATESIDE

STYLE: INDIA PALE ALE (IPA)

STATISTICS

Volume	20 litres (5⅓ gallons)
Boil volume	25 litres (6½ gallons)
OG	1072
BG	1058
FG	1017
Alcohol	6.9% abv
Colour	20 EBC
Bitterness	~100+ IBU

MASHING

Pilsner Malt	3 EBC	4550g (9lb 15oz)
Cara Munich I Malt	90 EBC	500g (1lb 2oz)
Munich I Malt	23 EBC	755g (1lb 10½oz)
Flaked Oats	4 EBC	755g (1lb 10½oz)
Total malt		6510g (14lb 5½oz)
Mashing programme		66°C (151°F) for 60 min

HOPS

Chinook	12.7% alpha	18g (½oz)	60 min
Amarillo	9.4% alpha	18g (½oz)	15 min
Cascade	5.7% alpha	12g (⅓oz)	15 min
Amarillo	9.4% alpha	12g (⅓oz)	1 min
Cascade	5.7% alpha	25g (1oz)	1 min

FERMENTATION

Yeast	Safale S-04
Temperature	19-21°C (66-70°F)

Mikkeller

Big Bad

Barley Wine

design vinther/clausen

Big Bad Barley Wine alc. 10,0%
Brygget af Mikkeller
Brygget af : Vand, malt,
amerikansk humle og
amerikansk gær.

Bør drikkes inden udgangen af 2005

BIG BAD BARLEY WINE

STYLE: BARLEY WINE

STATISTICS

Volume	20 litres (5⅓ gallons)
Boil volume	25 litres (6½ gallons)
OG	1105
BG	1084
FG	1028
Alcohol	10% abv
Colour	35 EBC
Bitterness	~100+ IBU

MASHING

Pale Malt	7 EBC	7700g (16lb 15½oz)
Cara Munich I Malt	100 EBC	1200g (2lb 10oz)
Total malt		8900g (19lb 10oz)
Mashing programme		70°C (158°F) for 60 min

HOPS

Nugget	2.8% alpha	110g (3¾oz)	60 min
Cascade	5.7% alpha	70g (2½oz)	1 min
Centennial	10.0% alpha	50g (1¾oz)	dry hop
Cascade	5.7% alpha	50g (1¾oz)	dry hop

FERMENTATION

Yeast	1056 American Ale
Temperature	20-22°C (68-72°F)

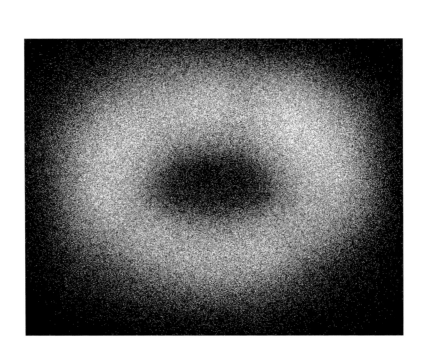

BLACK HOLE

STYLE: IMPERIAL STOUT

STATISTICS

Volume	20 litres (5⅓ gallons)
Boil volume	25 litres (6½ gallons)
OG	1118
BG	1094
FG	1023
Alcohol	13.1% abv
Colour	151 EBC
Bitterness	~100+ IBU

MASHING

Pilsner Malt	3 EBC	2400g (5lb 4½oz)
Flaked Mats	4 EBC	425g (15oz)
Pale Malt	7 EBC	2800g (6lb 3½oz)
Brown Malt	150 EBC	600g (1lb 5oz)
Chocolate Malt	940 EBC	400g (14oz)
Roasted Barley	1150 EBC	650g (1lb 7oz)

Total malt	7275g (16lbs)
Mashing programme	67°C (153°F) for 60 min

HOPS

Columbus	15.8% alpha	55g (2oz)	60 min
Chinook	13.0% alpha	25g (1oz)	60 min
Cascade	5.9% alpha	75g (2¾oz)	15 min
Amarillo	9.4% alpha	75g (2¾oz)	5 min

SUGAR

Brown Sugar	150 EBC	1500g (3lb 5oz)	15 min
Honey	40 EBC	300g (10½oz)	5 min

FERMENTATION

Yeast	1056 American Ale
Temperature	21-23°C (70-73°F)

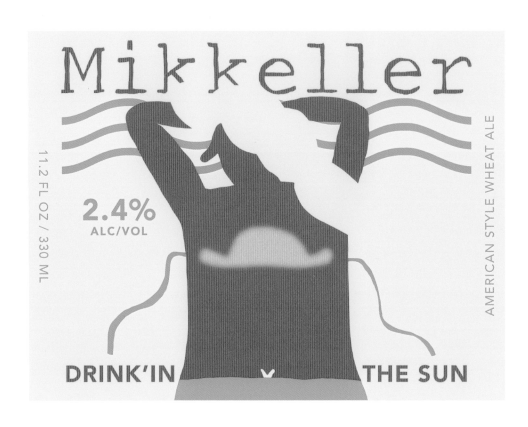

Mikkeller

2.4%
ALC/VOL

11.2 FL OZ / 330 ML

AMERICAN STYLE WHEAT ALE

DRINK'IN   THE SUN

DRINK'IN THE SUN

STYLE: AMERICAN WHEAT ALE

STATISTICS

Volume	20 litres (5⅓ gallons)
Boil volume	25 litres (6½ gallons)
OG	1028
BG	1023
FG	1010
Alcohol	2.4% abv
Colour	10 EBC
Bitterness	~38 IBU

MASHING

Pale Malt	7 EBC	1000g (2¼lb)
Wheat Malt	3 EBC	900g (1lb 15½oz)
Cara Red Malt	40 EBC	500g (1lb 2oz)
Total malt		2400g (5lb 4½oz)
Mashing programme		65°C (159°F) for 60 min

HOPS

Ahtanum	8.0% alpha	30g (1¼oz)	60 min
Tettnanger	3.8% alpha	25g (1oz)	1 min
Amarillo	8.0% alpha	50g (1¾oz)	1 min
Amarillo	8.0% alpha	50g (1¾oz)	dry hop
Tettnanger	3.8% alpha	25g (1oz)	dry hop

FERMENTATION

Yeast	WLP002 English Ale
Temperature	19-21°C (66-70°F)

AMERICAN-STYLE INDIA PALE ALE

GREEN

GOLD

Mikkeller

GREEN GOLD

STYLE: INDIA PALE ALE (IPA)

STATISTICS

Volume	20 litres (5⅓ gallons)
Boil volume	25 litres (6½ gallons)
OG	1067
BG	1053
FG	1014
Alcohol	7.0% abv
Colour	22 EBC
Bitterness	~100+ IBU

MASHING

Pilsner Malt	3 EBC	4200g (9lb ¼oz)
Cara Munich I Malt	100 EBC	600g (1lb 5oz)
Munich I Malt	23 EBC	600g (1lb 5oz)
Flaked Oats	4 EBC	600g (1lb 5oz)

Total malt	6000g (13lb ¼oz)
Mashing programme	66°C (151°F) for 60 min

HOPS

Simcoe	13.0% alpha	50g (1¾oz)	60 min
Cascade	6.0% alpha	20g (¾oz)	15 min
Amarillo	10.0% alpha	20g (¾oz)	1 min
Santiam	14.0% alpha	20g (¾oz)	dry hop
Amarillo	10.0% alpha	20g (¾oz)	dry hop

FERMENTATION

Yeast	WLP013 London Ale
Temperature	20-22°C (68-72°F)

Mikkeller

NAME

BROWN / JACKIE

ALC/VOL	INDHOLD
6.0%	**330 ml**

BREWED & BOTTLED BY **MIKKELLER**
AT   DE PROEF BROUWERIJ,
LOCHRISTI-HIJFTE, BELGIUM

 MINDST HOLDBAR TIL: SE KAPSEL

Øl. Ingredienser: vand, malt (Pale, Munich, Cara-Pils,
Cara-Crystal, Brown og Chocolate), havreflager, humle
(Nugget, Simcoe og Centennial) og ale gær.

Opbevares mørkt og køligt.

mikkeller.dk

5 704255 102896

JACKIE BROWN

STYLE: AMERICAN BROWN ALE

STATISTICS

Volume	20 litres (5⅓ gallons)
Boil volume	25 litres (6½ gallons)
OG	1063
BG	1051
FG	1017
Alcohol	6.0% abv
Colour	46 EBC
Bitterness	~77 IBU

MASHING

Pilsner Malt	4 EBC	3200g (7lb)
Munich I Malt	23 EBC	600g (1lb 5oz)
Cara Crystal Malt	110 EBC	400g (14oz)
Flaked Oats	5 EBC	600g (1lb 5oz)
Brown Malt	150 EBC	600g (1lb 5oz)
Chocolate (dehusked)	1000 EBC	100g (3½oz)
Cara Pils Malt	4 EBC	200g (7oz)

Total malt	5700g (12½lbs)
Mashing programme	65°C (149°F) for 60 min

HOPS

Nugget	13.0% alpha	35g (1¼oz)	60 min
Centennial	10.0% alpha	35g (1¼oz)	5 min
Amarillo	9.4% alpha	35g (1¼oz)	dry hop

FERMENTATION

Yeast	1028 London Ale
Temperature	19-20°C (66-68°F)

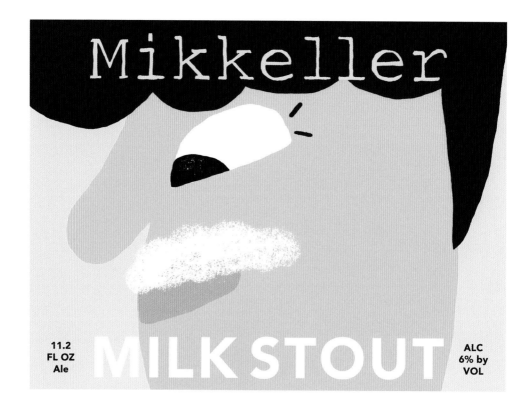

Mikkeller

11.2
FL OZ
Ale

MILK STOUT

ALC
6% by
VOL

MILK STOUT

STYLE: SWEET STOUT

STATISTICS

Volume	20 litres (5⅓ gallons)
Boil volume	25 litres (6½ gallons)
OG	1076
BG	1061
FG	1030
Alcohol	6.0% abv
Colour	98 EBC
Bitterness	~39 IBU

MASHING

Maris Otter Pale Malt	5 EBC	2800g (6lb 3oz)	
Flaked Mats	4 EBC	1300g (2lb 14oz)	
Pale Chocolate Malt	500 EBC	450g (1lb)	
Chocolate Malt	900 EBC	600g (1lb 5oz)	

Total malt	5150g (11lb 5½oz)
Mashing programme	67°C (152°F) for 60 min

HOPS

Columbus	16.0% alpha	15g (½oz)	60 min
Cascade	6.5% alpha	5g (⅛oz)	15 min
Amarillo	6.5% alpha	5g (⅛oz)	5 min
Centennial	10.0% alpha	10g (¼oz)	1 min

SUGAR

Lactose	0 EBC	950g (2lb 1½oz)	15 min

FERMENTATION

Yeast	WLP002 English Ale
Temperature	19-21 °C (66-70°F)

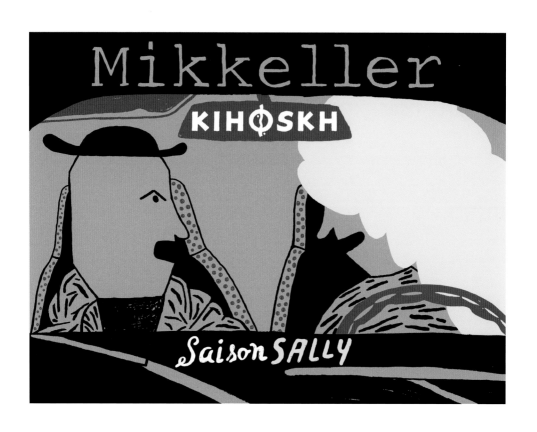

SAISON SALLY

STYLE: SAISON

STATISTICS

Volume	20 litres (5⅓ gallons)
Boil volume	25 litres (6½ gallons)
OG	1062
BG	1050
FG	1010
Alcohol	6.8% abv
Colour	7 EBC
Bitterness	~19 IBU

MASHING

Pale Malt	3 EBC	4000g (8lb 3oz)
Wheat Malt	3 EBC	475g (1lb 1oz)
Vienna Malt	7 EBC	250g (9oz)

Total malt	4725g (10lb 6½oz)
Mashing programme	65°C (149°F) for 60 min

HOPS

Styrian Golding	4.0% alpha	25g (1oz)	60 min
East Kent Golding	4.4% alpha	12g (⅓oz)	60 min
East Kent Goldin	4.4% alpha	8g (⅛oz)	15 min
Saaz	2.8% alpha	8g (⅛oz)	5 min

SUGAR

Kandis (light)	0 EBC	425g (15oz)	15 min

FERMENTATION

Yeast	WLP565 Belgian Saison I Yeast
Temperature	32-35°C (90-95°F)

COMMENTS

15g (½oz) bitter orange peel added to the hops for the final 15 min of boiling.

VESTERBRO PILSNER

STYLE: AMERICAN LAGER

STATISTICS

Volume	20 litres (5⅓ gallons)
Boil volume	25 litres (6½ gallons)
OG	1054
BG	1043
FG	1012
Alcohol	5.6% abv
Colour	12 EBC
Bitterness	~43 IBU

MASHING

Pilsner Malt	4 EBC	2900g (6lb 6⅓oz)
Munich I Malt	23 EBC	950g (2lb 1½oz)
Cara Pils Malt	5 EBC	950g (2lb 1½oz)
Total malt		4800g (10lb 9⅓oz)
Mashing programme		66°C (151°F) for 60 min

HOPS

Zeus	12.8% alpha	20g (¾oz)	60 min
Nelson Sauvin	12.0% alpha	40g (1¼oz)	1 min
Cascade	6.5% alpha	40g (1¼oz)	1 min
Simcoe	13.0% alpha	40g (1¼oz)	dry hop
Amarillo	6.5% alpha	40g (1¼oz)	dry hop

FERMENTATION

Yeast	2124 Bohemian Lager
Temperature	11-13°C (52-55°F)

Mikkeller

BIG TONY 2006

En IIIPA på 15.0% vol.
og 500+ IBU.

Brygget af Mikkeller.

Brygget på:
vand, malt (pale og amber),
rørsukker, humle (warrior,
vanguard, columbus, chinook,
willamette, cascade og nugget)
og high gravity gær.

BIG TONY

STYLE: BARLEY WINE

STATISTICS

Volume	20 litres (5⅓ gallons)
Boil volume	25 litres (6½ gallons)
OG	1140
BG	1112
FG	1025
Alcohol	15.0% abv
Colour	21 EBC
Bitterness	~100+ IBU

MASHING

Pale Malt	6 EBC	7200g (15lb 14oz)
Amber Malt	100 EBC	375g (13oz)
Total malt		7575g (16lb 11oz)
Mashing programme		65°C (149°F) for 60 min

HOPS

Chinook	12.6% alpha	160g (5½oz)	90 min
Columbus	16.0% alpha	177g (6¼oz)	15 min
Williamette	7.5% alpha	88g (3oz)	1 min
Cascade	5.7% alpha	44g (1½oz)	1 min
Columbus	16.0% alpha	10g (¼oz)	dry hop

SUGAR

Glucose	0 EBC	2500g (5½lb)	15 min

FERMENTATION

Yeast	1056 American Ale
Temperature	21-23°C (70-73°F)

Mikkeller MONK'S BREW

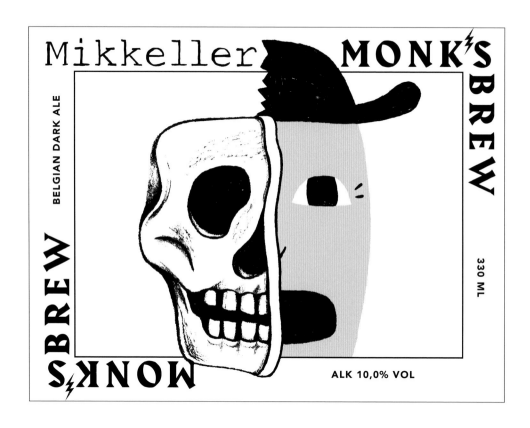

BELGIAN DARK ALE

BREW

MONK'S

330 ML

ALK 10,0% VOL

MONK'S BREW

STYLE: DARK STRONG BELGIAN ALE

STATISTICS

Volume	20 litres (5⅓ gallons)
Boil volume	25 litres (6½ gallons)
OG	1090
BG	1072
FG	1013
Alcohol	10.0% abv
Colour	59 EBC
Bitterness	~36 IBU

MASHING

Pilsner Malt	3 EBC	2900g (6lb 6⅓oz)	
Pale Malt	7 EBC	2900g (6lb 6⅓oz)	
Total malt		5800g (12lb 12½oz)	
Mashing programme		67°C (153°F) for 60 min	

HOPS

Northern Brewer	8.9% alpha	17g (½oz)	60 min
Hallertauer	3.4% alpha	31g (1oz)	30 min
Styrian Golding	4.4% alpha	19g (½oz)	30 min

SUGAR

Brown Sugar	150 EBC	575g (1¼lb)	15 min
Candy Sugar (Dark)	425 EBC	600g (1lb oz)	15 min

FERMENTATION

Yeast	3787 Belgian Trappist
Temperature	28-30°C (82-86°F)

Mikkeller

DR4FT BEAR

8% Alk   IMPERIAL PILSNER   330 ml

DRAFT BEAR

STYLE: IMPERIAL PILSNER

STATISTICS

Volume	20 litres (5⅓ gallons)
Boil volume	25 litres (6½ gallons)
OG	1073
BG	1058
FG	1012
Alcohol	8.0% abv
Colour	13 EBC
Bitterness	~90 IBU

MASHING

Pilsner Malt	3 EBC	4330g (6½lb)
Cara Pils Malt	20 EBC	665g (1lb 7½oz)
Amber Malt	50 EBC	330g (11½oz)
Total malt		5325g (11¾lb)
Mashing programme		66°C (151°F) for 60 min

HOPS

Amarillo	9.0% alpha	50g (1¾oz)	60 min
Cascade	6.0% alpha	50g (1¾oz)	15 min
Cascade	6.0% alpha	50g (1¾oz)	5 min
Amarillo	9.0% alpha	31g (1oz)	dry hop
Cascade	6.0% alpha	31g (1oz)	dry hop

SUGAR

Candy Sugar (Light)	0 EBC	650g (1lb 7oz)	10 min

FERMENTATION

Yeast	Saflager S-23
Temperature	12-13°C (53-55°F)

Mikkeller

Humlefryyyd

En 'American Strong Ale'
på 9,0% vol.

Brygget af Mikkeller.

Brygget på:
vand, malt, humle og gær.

Brygget til Ølbaren, KBH, Denmark

HUMLEFRYYYD

STYLE: INDIA PALE ALE

STATISTICS

Volume	20 litres (5⅓ gallons)
Boil volume	25 litres (6½ gallons)
OG	1086
BG	1069
FG	1018
Alcohol	9.0% abv
Colour	23 EBC
Bitterness	~100+ IBU

MASHING

Pale Malt	5 EBC	6500g (14lb 5½oz)
Flaked Oats	4 EBC	250g (9oz)
Cara Crystal Malt	120 EBC	400g (14oz)
Cara Munich I Malt	90 EBC	125g (4½oz)

Total malt	5150g (11lb 5½oz)
Mashing programme	67°C (152°F) for 60 min

HOPS

Simcoe	13.0% alpha	60g (2oz)	60 min
Centennial	11.0% alpha	45g (1½oz)	60 min
Cascade	5.7% alpha	65g (2⅓oz)	30 min
Amarillo	9.5% alpha	50g (1¾oz)	15 min
Cascade	5.7% alpha	65g (2⅓oz)	1 min
Cascade	5.7% alpha	100g (3½oz)	dry hop
Simcoe	13.0% alpha	100g (3½oz)	dry hop

FERMENTATION

Yeast	1056 American Ale
Temperature	20-22°C (68-72°F)

Mikkeller!

Mindst holdbar til (Best Before):

Brewed & Bottled by **Mikkeller**
at BrewDog, Ellon, Scotland

Øl. Ingredienser: vand, malt,
flækket havre, humle og gær.

Imported to the US
by **Shelton Brothers**
Belchertown, MA

Product of Scotland
9.75% ALC/VOL

Mikkeller.dk

330
ml℮

Mikkeller

I
Beat
yoU.

11.2
FL OZ

An American-Style
Imperial India Pale Ale.

I BEAT YOU

STYLE: INDIA PALE ALE

STATISTICS

Volume	20 litres (5⅓ gallons)
Boil volume	25 litres (6½ gallons)
OG	1089
BG	1071
FG	1015
Alcohol	9.75% abv
Colour	29 EBC
Bitterness	~100+ IBU

MASHING

Maris Otter Pale Malt	5 EBC	4953g	(10lb 14¾oz)
Cara Munich I Malt	90 EBC	933g	(2lb)
Munich I Malt	23 EBC	861g	(1lb 14⅓oz)
Flaked Oats	4 EBC	933g	(2lb)

Total malt		7680g (16lb 15oz)
Mashing programme		67°C (152°F) for 60 min

HOPS

Chinook	12.6% alpha	90g (3oz)	60 min
Centennial	9.0% alpha	10g (¼oz)	30 min
Simcoe	13.1% alpha	10g (¼oz)	30 min
Amarillo	9.1% alpha	10g (¼oz)	30 min
Centennial	9.0% alpha	10g (¼oz)	10 min
Simcoe	13.1% alpha	10g (¼oz)	10 min
Amarillo	9.1% alpha	10g (¼oz)	10 min
Centennial	9.0% alpha	10g (¼oz)	1 min
Simcoe	13.1% alpha	10g (¼oz)	1 min
Amarillo	9.1% alpha	10g (¼oz)	1 min
Centennial	9.0% alpha	10g (¼oz)	dry hop
Simcoe	13.1% alpha	10g (¼oz)	dry hop
Columbus	14.5% alpha	50g (1¾oz)	dry hop

FERMENTATION

Yeast	1056 American Ale
Temperature	20-22°C (68-72°F)

TEXAS
RANGER
CHIPOTLE PORTER

Mikkeller

TEXAS RANGER

STYLE: PORTER

STATISTICS

Volume	20 litres (5⅓ gallons)
Boil volume	25 litres (6½ gallons)
OG	1086
BG	1069
FG	1036
Alcohol	6.6% abv
Colour	166 EBC
Bitterness	~68 IBU

MASHING

Maris Otter Pale Malt	5 EBC	4500g (9lb 15oz)
Chocolate Malt	800 EBC	768g (1lb 11oz)
Roasted Barley	1100 EBC	768g (1lb 11oz)
Cara Crystal Malt	130 EBC	960g (2lb 2oz)
Brown Malt	150 EBC	672g (1lb 8oz)

Total malt	7668g (16lb 14½oz)
Mashing programme	68°C (154°F) for 60 min

HOPS

Columbus	16.0% alpha	25g (1oz)	60 min
Saaz	2.8% alpha	32g (1oz)	15 min
Centennial	10.0% alpha	64g (2¼oz)	1 min

FERMENTATION

Yeast	1056 American Ale
Temperature	20-22°C (68-72°F)

COMMENTS

15g (½oz) chipotle chili powder added for the final 10 min of boiling.

Øl. Ingredienser: vand, malt (pilsner,
munich og cara-pils), humle (saaz,
hallertauer, spalt og tettnanger) og
lagergær.

Indhold: 330 ml. Alk. 4.6% vol.
Holdbar til: Se kapsel
Se mere på: www.mikkeller.dk
Brygget på De Proef Brouwerij, Belgien.

TJEKKET PILSNER

STYLE: CZECH PILSNER

STATISTICS

Volume	20 litres (5⅓ gallons)
Boil volume	25 litres (6½ gallons)
OG	1047
BG	1038
FG	1011
Alcohol	4.6% abv
Colour	9 EBC
Bitterness	~36 IBU

MASHING

Pilsner Malt	4 EBC	3530g (7lb 12½oz)
Munich I Malt	23 EBC	330g (11½oz)
Cara Pils Malt	5 EBC	330g (11½oz)
Total malt		4190g (9lb 3½oz)
Mashing programme		65°C (149°F) for 60 min

HOPS

Zeus	13.0% alpha	15g (½oz)	60 min
Saaz	3.1% alpha	20g (¾oz)	30 min
Saaz	3.1% alpha	25g (1oz)	10 min
Saaz	3.1% alpha	60g (2oz)	dry hop

FERMENTATION

Yeast	2124 Bohemian Lager
Temperature	11-13°C (52-55°F)

COMMENTS

A little diacetyl is okay.

Mikkeller

SIMCOE SINGLE HOP IPA

ØL. INGREDIENSER: VAND, MALT
(PILSNER, CARA-CRYSTAL OG
MUNICH), HAVREFLAGER, HUMLE
(SIMCOE) OG GÆR.

BRYGGET PÅ DE PROEF BROUWERIJ, BELGIEN.
SE MERE PÅ MIKKELLER.DK
INDHOLD: 330 ML. ALK. 6,9% VOL. HOLDBARHED: SE KAPSEL

SIMCOE SINGLE HOP IPA

STYLE: INDIA PALE ALE

STATISTICS

Volume	20 litres (5⅓ gallons)
Boil volume	25 litres (6½ gallons)
OG	1063
BG	1051
FG	1010
Alcohol	6.9% abv
Colour	22 EBC
Bitterness	~100+ IBU

MASHING

Pilsner Malt	3 EBC	3800g (8lb 6oz)
Cara Crystal Malt	120 EBC	500g (1lb 2oz)
Munich I Malt	22 EBC	675g (1lb ½oz)
Flaked Oats	4 EBC	600g (1lb 5oz)

Total malt	5575g (12lb 5oz)
Mashing programme	67°C (153°F) for 60 min

HOPS

Simcoe	13.0% alpha	60g (2oz)	60 min
Simcoe	13.0% alpha	60g (2oz)	15 min
Simcoe	13.0% alpha	60g (2oz)	1 min
Simcoe	13.0% alpha	40g (1½oz)	dry hop

FERMENTATION

Yeast	1056 American Ale
Temperature	19-21°C (66-70°F)

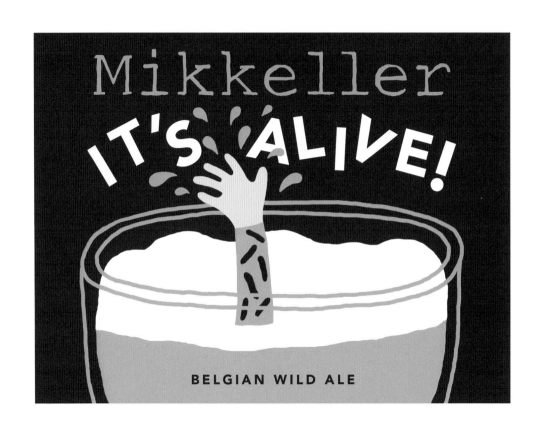

IT'S ALIVE!

STYLE: BELGIAN WILD ALE

STATISTICS

Volume	20 litres (5⅓ gallons)
Boil volume	25 litres (6½ gallons)
OG	1065
BG	1052
FG	1004
Alcohol	8.0% abv
Colour	20 EBC
Bitterness	~60 IBU

MASHING

Pale Malt	7 EBC	3650g (8lb)
Cara I Munich	90 EBC	585g (1¼lb)
Total malt		4235g (9lb 5oz)
Mashing programme		64°C (140°F) for 60 min

HOPS

Zeus	13.0% alpha	15g (½oz)	60 min
Saaz	3.1% alpha	20g (¾oz)	30 min
Saaz	3.1% alpha	25g (1oz)	10 min
Saaz	3.1% alpha	60g (2oz)	dry hop

SUGAR

Candy Sugar (Light)	0 EBC	750g (1lb 10½oz)	5 min

FERMENTATION

Yeast	WLP510 Bastogne Belgian Ale Yeast Brettanomyces brux
Temperature	23-24°C (73-75°F)

Mikkeller
Red/White Christmas

Holdbar til

Tappet 10 år før

Indhold: 1500 ml.
Alc: 8.0% vol.
Opbevares mørkt og køligt.

Pant C

En imperial red/white ale
brygget på: vand, malt (pale,
vienna, og cara-red), umalted
hvede, flækket hvede, humle
(tomahawk, saaz, simcoe og
amarillo), krydderier (curacao
appelsinskal og korianderfrø),
witbier-gær og alegær.

Se mere på www.mikkeller.dk.

RED WHITE CHRISTMAS

STYLE: RED ALE/WITBIER HYBRID

STATISTICS

Volume	20 litres (5⅓ gallons)
Boil volume	25 litres (6½ gallons)
OG	1079
BG	1063
FG	1018
Alcohol	8.0% abv
Colour	19 EBC
Bitterness	~91 IBU

MASHING

Vienne Malt	7 EBC	1710g (3¾lb)
Cara Red Malt	40 EBC	855g (1lb 14oz)
Pale Malt	7 EBC	2570g (5lb 11oz)
Flaked Wheat	3 EBC	340g (12oz)
Unmalted Wheat	3 EBC	1370g (3lb)
Total malt		6845g (15lb 1oz)
Mashing programme	69°C (156°F) for 60 min

HOPS

Columbus	16.0% alpha	30g (1oz)	60 min
Saaz	2.8% alpha	35g (1¼oz)	15 min
Simcoe	13.0% alpha	35g (1¼oz)	5 min
Tomahawk	15.8% alpha	35g (1¼oz)	1 min
Amarillo	6.5% alpha	71g (2½oz)	dry hop

FERMENTATION

Yeast	1056 American Ale
Temperature	21-22°C (70-72°F)

COMMENTS

20g (¾oz) Curaçao orange peel and 20g (¾oz) ground coriander seeds added to the hops for the final 15 min of boiling.

WEIZENBOCK

STYLE: WEIZENBOCK

STATISTICS

Volume	20 litres (5⅓ gallons)
Boil volume	25 litres (6½ gallons)
OG	1083
BG	1066
FG	1018
Alcohol	8.5% abv
Colour	20 EBC
Bitterness	~17 IBU

MASHING

Wheat Malt	3 EBC	3550g (7lb 13oz)
Munich I Malt	20 EBC	1330g (2lb 15oz)
Pilsner Malt	3 EBC	1330g (2lb 15oz)
Cara Red Malt	3 EBC	885g (1lb 15oz)

Total malt	7095g (15lb 10oz)
Mashing programme	70°C (158°F) for 60 min

HOPS

Hallertauer	6.6% alpha	17g (½oz)	60 min
Hallertauer	6.6% alpha	4g (⅛oz)	15 min

FERMENTATION

Yeast	WLP300 Hefeweizen Ale
Temperature	21-23°C (70-73°F)

PORTER

STYLE: PORTER

STATISTICS

Volume	20 litres (5⅓ gallons)
Boil volume	25 litres (6½ gallons)
OG	1084
BG	1068
FG	1028
Alcohol	7.4% abv
Colour	115 EBC
Bitterness	~72 IBU

MASHING

Maris Otter Pale Malt	5 EBC	5000g (11⅓lb)
Chocolate Malt	800 EBC	425g (15oz)
Roasted Barley	1100 EBC	425g (15oz)
Cara Crystal Malt	130 EBC	425g (15oz)
Brown Malt	200 EBC	425g (15oz)
Smoked Malt	6 EBC	210g (7¼oz)

Total malt	6910g (15lb 3¼oz)
Mashing programme	68°C (154°F) for 60 min

HOPS

Columbus	16.0% alpha	16g (½oz)	90 min
Amarillo	6.5% alpha	16g (½oz)	90 min
Saaz	2.8% alpha	16g (½oz)	30 min
Columbus	16.0% alpha	16g (½oz)	15 min
Amarillo	6.5% alpha	16g (½oz)	1 min

SUGAR

Brown Sugar	80 EBC	240g (8½oz)	10 min

FERMENTATION

Yeast	WLP002 English Ale
Temperature	121-123°C (70-73°F)

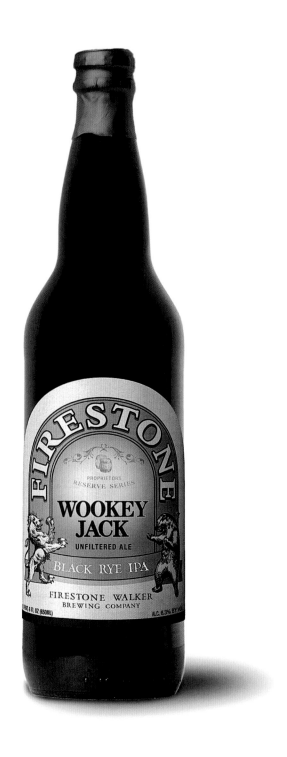

WOOKEY JACK

STYLE: BLACK IPA

STATISTICS

Volume	20 litres (5⅓ gallons)
Boil volume	25 litres (6½ gallons)
OG	1074
BG	1059
FG	1011
Alcohol	8.3% abv
Colour	47 EBC
Bitterness	~54 IBU

MASHING

Pale Malt	7 EBC	4753g (10lb 7oz)
Rye Malt	6 EBC	451g (1lb)
Cara-Rye Malt	100 EBC	149g (5¼oz)
Carafe III Malt	1220 EBC	179g (6⅓oz)
Light Wheat Malt	3 EBC	179g (6⅓oz)

Total malt	5711g (12lb 9½oz)
Mashing programme	63°C (145°F) for 45 min
	68°C (154°F) for 15 min
	74°C (165°F) for 10 min

FIRESTONE WALKER

California, USA.

Founded in 1996 by brothers-in-law Adam Firestone and David Walker.

Famous for its 'Firestone Union System' – a wooden barrel fermentation method inspired by an old English tradition – and, thanks to brewmaster Matthew Brynildson, for hitting the mark when it comes to brewing classic beer types.

A four-times World Beer Cup Champion Brewery in the mid-size brewing company category.

Produced the Lil' Mikkel sour ale in collaboration with Mikkeller.

HOPS

Amarillo	6.5% alpha	15g (½oz)	60 min
Citra	11.0% alpha	15g (½oz)	60 min
Amarillo	6.5% alpha	10g (¼oz)	30 min
Citra	11.0% alpha	10g (¼oz)	30 min
Amarillo	6.5% alpha	10g (¼oz)	10 min
Amarillo	6.5% alpha	10g (¼oz)	10 min
Citra	11.0% alpha	38g (1⅓oz)	1 min
Amarillo	6.5% alpha	38g (1⅓oz)	1 min

SUGAR

Glucose	0 EBC	350g (12⅓oz)	10 min

FERMENTATION

Yeast	1028 London Ale
Temperature	Start at 19°C (66°F), increase to 21°C (70°F) at gravity 1024

THE KERNEL BREWERY LONDON

- - -   - - -

IMPERIAL BROWN STOUT
LONDON 1856

10.1% ABV

- - -   - - -

IMPERIAL BROWN STOUT

STYLE: IMPERIAL STOUT

THE KERNEL

London, United Kingdom.

Founded by former cheese shop owner and home brewer, Irishman Evin O'Riordain, in 2009.

Famous for bringing highly hopped Americans IPAs to the United Kingdom.

Planning a collaborative beer with Mikkeller.

STATISTICS

Volume	20 litres (5⅓ gallons)
Boil volume	25 litres (6½ gallons)
OG	1101
BG	1081
FG	1025
Alcohol	10.1% abv
Colour	100 EBC
Bitterness	~100+ IBU

HOPS

Magnum	14.0% alpha	30g (1oz)	90 min
Apollo	19.0% alpha	9g (⅛oz)	90 min
Nugget	13.0% alpha	12g (⅓oz)	90 min
Columbus	16.0% alpha	9g (⅛oz)	90 min

SUGAR

Brown Sugar	20 EBC	694g (1½lb)	10 min

MASHING

Pale Malt	7 EBC	5382g (11lb 14oz)
Brown Malt	150 EBC	705g (1lb 8½oz)
Black Malt	1100 EBC	562g (1¼lb)
Munich I Malt	23 EBC	705g (1lb 8½oz)
Amber Malt	69 EBC	228g (8oz)

Total malt	7582g (16lb 11½oz)
Mashing programme	67°C (153°F) for 60 min

FERMENTATION

Yeast	1028 London Ale
Temperature	19-21°C (66-70°F)

BREWED & BOTTLED BY THREE FLOYDS BREWING LLC, MUNSTER, IN

GOVERNMENT WARNING: (1) ACCORDING TO THE SURGEON GENERAL, WOMEN SHOULD NOT DRINK ALCOHOLIC BEVERAGES DURING PREGNANCY BECAUSE OF THE RISK OF BIRTH DEFECTS. (2) CONSUMPTION OF ALCOHOLIC BEVERAGES IMPAIRS YOUR ABILITY TO DRIVE A CAR OR OPERATE MACHINERY, AND MAY CAUSE HEALTH PROBLEMS

CA CASH REFUND
CT • ME • VT • MA MI 10¢
NY-IA-OR-DE 5¢ REFUND

1 PINT 6 FL OZ

LABEL: ZIMMER-DESIGN.COM

DREAD-DOUBLE IPA

STYLE: IMPERIAL INDIA PALE ALE (IIPA)

THREE FLOYDS

Munster, Indiana, USA.

Founded by brothers Nick and Simon Floyd and their father Mike in 1996.

Rated #1 brewer in the world by ratebeer.com on multiple occasions.

Famous for its heavy metal image and its 'Dark Lord' Russian imperial stout.

Holds the annual 'Dark Lord Day' festival in the last weekend in April.

Produced a number of collaborative beers with Mikkeller.

STATISTICS

Volume	20 litres (5⅓ gallons)
Boil volume	25 litres (6½ gallons)
OG	1098
BG	1078
FG	1030
Alcohol	9.0% abv
Colour	19 EBC
Bitterness	~100+ IBU

HOPS

Simcoe	13.0% alpha	28g (1oz)	90 min
Warrior	8.3% alpha	28g (1oz)	60 min
Centennial	10.0% alpha	14g (½oz)	90 min
Centennial	10.0% alpha	14g (½oz)	45 min
Centennial	10.0% alpha	14g (½oz)	30 min
Centennial	10.0% alpha	28g (1oz)	5 min
Centennial	10.0% alpha	56g (2oz)	1 min
Cascade	8.0% alpha	56g (2oz)	dry hop
Centennial	10.0% alpha	56g (2oz)	dry hop

MASHING

Pilsner Malt	3 EBC	7615g (16lb 12½oz)
Melanoidin Malt	69 EBC	650g (1lb 7oz)
Wheat Malt	3 EBC	420g (15oz)

Total malt	8685g (19lb 2oz)
Mashing programme	67-68°C (153-155°F) for 60 min

FERMENTATION

Yeast	1968 Special London Ale
Temperature	19-20°C (66-68°F)

TO
ØL

GOLIAT
IMPERIAL STOUT

GOLIAT

STYLE: IMPERIAL STOUT

TO ØL

Copenhagen, Denmark.

Founded by school friends Tobias Emil Jensen and Tore Gynther in 2010.

Taught to brew at the Det frie Gymnasium (Free Upper Secondary School) by Mikkel, who was teaching there at the time.

Famous for its highly hopped reinterpretations of classic beer types, including the 'Reparationsbajer' pale ale.

Co-owner of the Nørrebro bar Mikkeller & Friends.

STATISTICS

Volume	20 litres (5⅓ gallons)
Boil volume	25 litres (6½ gallons)
OG	1105
BG	1084
FG	1028
Alcohol	10.1% abv
Colour	161 EBC
Bitterness	~100+ IBU

MASHING

Pilsner Malt	3 EBC	5417g (11lb 15oz)
Smoked Malt	6 EBC	571g (1¼lb)
Chocolate Malt	800 EBC	685g (1½lb)
Roasted Barley	1100 EBC	800g (1lb 12oz)
Cara Crystal Malt	120 EBC	457g (1lb 1oz)
Aroma Malt	150 EBC	411g (14½oz)
Flaked Oats	4 EBC	800g (1¾lb)

Total malt	9141g (20lb 2½oz)
Mashing programme	65°C (149°F) for 60 min

HOPS

Columbus	16.0% alpha	50g (1¾oz)	60 min
Columbus	16.0% alpha	53g (2oz)	10 min
Simcoe	13.0% alpha	53g (2oz)	1 min

SUGAR

Dark Brown Sugar	80 EBC	622g (1lb 6oz)	15 min

FERMENTATION

Yeast	WLP001 California Ale
Temperature	19-21°C (66-70°F)

COMMENTS

0.5 litres (1 pint) press coffee made with 60g (2oz) coffee added a few days before bottling.

Hemel & Aarde

Original handcrafted beer

| 24° Plato | www.brouwerijdemolen.nl | EBC 342 108 EBU |

Ingredients: water, munich, cara, brown and bruichladdich barley malts, premiant and sladek (late hopping), yeast (top fermenting).

Enjoy within 25 years. Keep cool and dark.
Brewed and bottled in Bodegraven.
Recommended drinking temperature 10 °C.

please drink responsibly
bottled on: see back label
no deposit please recycle

unpasteurized

10%ALC/VOL 75cl

8 717624 421020

BROUWERIJ
DE MOLEN

HEMEL &AARDE

STYLE: IMPERIAL STOUT

STATISTICS

Volume	20 litres (5⅓ gallons)
Boil volume	25 litres (6½ gallons)
OG	1102
BG	1081
FG	1024
Alcohol	10.0% abv
Colour	342 EBC (Black)
Bitterness	~100+ IBU

MASHING

Pale Malt	7 EBC	5133g (11lb 5oz)
Cara Crystal Malt	120 EBC	1026g (2¼lb)
Aroma Malt (Bruichladdich)	120 EBC	1026g (2¼lb)
Peated Malt	5 EBC	1026g (2¼lb)
Roasted Barley	1200 EBC	533g (1lb 3oz)

Total malt	8744g (19¼lb)
Mashing programme	52°C (127°F) for 15 min
	62°C (144°F) for 30 min
	72°C (162°F) for 30 min
	78°C (172°F) for 5 min

BROUWERIJ DE MOLEN

Bodegraven, Netherlands.

Founded by brewer Menno Olivier in 2004.

Famous for its imperial stouts.

Holds the annual Borefts Beer Festival in October.

Brewed the 'Mikkel & Menno' weisenbock in collaboration with Mikkeller.

HOPS

Premiant	8.2% alpha	120g (4⅓oz)	90 min
Sladek	5.4% alpha	80g (3oz)	10 min

FERMENTATION

Yeast	1028 London Ale
Temperature	21°C (70°F)

STATESIDE

This hoppy IPA is the first commercial beer that Mikkeller ever brewed. I created it with Keller in 2006, and the beer proved to be something of a challenge for us because it was the first home brew that we transferred to a large brewing facility. At the time, we were brewing at Ørbæk Brewery, and their facility simply couldn't take all the hops we had intended for the beer, so we had to get Pernille to sew a stack of huge hop bags from cheesecloth that we bought from the fabric store Stof 2000. The beer was also fermented in open fermentation tanks, which would never be done at a modern brewery today.

DRINK'IN THE SNOW

Over several years, we worked hard to produce our alcohol-free beer Drink'in the Sun, and we were so pleased with the result that we decided to make an alcohol-free Christmas beer as well. There are many people who, for one reason or another, cannot drink alcohol. As an example, Pernille really appreciated this beer last Christmas, when she was heavily pregnant. By comparison with Drink'in the Sun, which is a refreshing, hoppy summer beer, Drink'in the Snow is, logically enough, a sweeter, darker and maltier version.

BEER GEEK BRUNCH

Beer Geek Brunch was the follow-up to our classic Beer Geek Breakfast, which has a very special place in the history of Mikkeller as it was this beer that provided us with our breakthrough through on the international beer stage. The brunch version is made with a unique coffee from Vietnam that I came across during a trip many years ago. The special thing about this coffee is that it has passed through the stomach of a civet (a weasel-like animal), which eats the red coffee cherries. During the process, the coffee is fermented by the animal's digestive enzymes and ends up with a taste and smell all of its own – all the bitterness has gone and for the most part only thick chocolate notes remain. Subsequently, we also made Beer Geek Bacon, which has smoky characteristics, Beer Hop Breakfast, with extra hops, and Beer Geek Vanilla Shake, a sweet dessert-like version of the beer.

SPONTAN CHERRY FREDERIKSDAL

Several years ago, I became acquainted with Frederiksdal's cherry wine. The wine is made by three passionate souls who grow their own cherries in orchards at Frederiksdal Manor on the island of Lolland. It is without doubt the best wine produced in Denmark, and in fact one of the finest Danish products of all. In 2013, we came together to produce this beer, which consists of equal parts of cherry juice and beer fermented for seven months. I am very, very pleased with the result and would go so far as to say it was the best new beer we made at Mikkeller in 2013.

NELSON SAUVIGNON

This beer is one of my personal favourites. Conceived as a New Year's Eve beer counterpart to champagne, it was brewed with Nelson Sauvin hops, named after the Sauvignon Blanc grape variety becaue of their grape-like character. We also fermented it with champagne yeast, used enzymes to make it drier, and finally barrel-aged it – for the first year in Sauvignon Blanc barrels and then in Chardonnay barrels. The beer also has a high carbonic acid content like champagne.

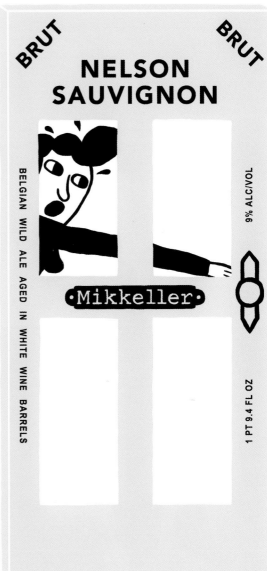

BRUT

BRUT

NELSON SAUVIGNON

BELGIAN WILD ALE AGED IN WHITE WINE BARRELS

·Mikkeller·

9% ALC/VOL

1 PT 9.4 FL OZ

CHAPTER 8

EAT AND DRINK ABOUT BEER AND FOOD

I love wine and I drink at least as much wine as beer with my food both at home and when I eat out. In fact, I have a wine cooler that is stuffed full, whereas I often forget to take beer home with me. When I started partnering with various chefs and restaurants, my ambition was not therefore to outcompete wine, but simply to establish that beer isn't just for enjoying with burgers and hot dogs but, like wine, it can be a powerful supplement to gourmet food and, because of its extremely broad range, even add a few things that wine can't offer.

Wine is made from one ingredient. It can be red, white, rosé or sparkling, and as a rule it has an alcohol content of 11–15% abv. There are obviously many nuances within these categories and many departures from them, but generally speaking that's what you have to work with. If you go out to eat at a modern gourmet restaurant, you will usually be served seven glasses of white wine and one glass of red. Wine aficionados can obviously taste the difference between the seven white wines, but the vast majority of people sit and wonder what distinguishes one from another. A beer, by contrast, can pack in just about anything, varying from fresh and hoppy at 3% abv to burnt and black at 6% abv. And then there is everything in between: spices, sweetness, fruit, sourness, etc. This range gives you a lot to work with when it comes to food.

My story of beer and food goes back to 2009, when I was contacted by a wine importer I knew, Herluf Trolle. In connection with the Copenhagen Cooking theme week, he had come up with the idea of holding an event where wine would compete against beer. It was to be arranged in collaboration with the Kiin Kiin Thai restaurant in Copenhagen, which had won its first Michelin star the previous year.

The contest was called 'Wine vs Beer'and with each of the 11 dishes the guests were served a glass of wine and a glass of beer. Herluf and I had tried out the menu in advance, and during each course we presented the beer and the wine that we had chosen to accompany the spicy Thai dishes. After each course, the guests were invited to record on a voting slip whether they preferred the beer or the wine.

Even before we started, it was clear that Henrik Yde-Andersen, sommelier and owner of Kiin Kiin, didn't really care much for beer. He was convinced that wine would thrash beer in the contest, but that's not how it turned out. The wine did win, but nowhere near as convincingly as he had expected. This opened his eyes to beer as a worthy supplement to gourmet food, and we subsequently entered into an agreement where Mikkeller began brewing special beers for all his restaurants. This whetted my appetite. If Henrik Yde-Andersen could change his opinion of beer, so too could many other chefs.

The next year, in May 2010, I opened Mikkeller Bar in Viktoriagade, Copenhagen. The bar gave me a shop window for Mikkeller's beer – a place where people could be invited to tastings. And I thought it might be exciting to try altering the fact that it was always wine that was preferred with gourmet food. Restaurants that had the craziest wine cellars containing the world's best wines could only just about manage to serve a Jacobsen from Carlsberg. That needed to change. I therefore invited all the staff from three of Copenhagen's leading restaurants – Noma, Mielcke & Hurtigkarl and Kiin Kiin – to the bar for a beer tasting.

This resulted in a number of partnerships, one of the most rewarding being that with the chef Jakob Mielcke from Mielcke & Hurtigkarl. He is essentially open to anything new and not stuck in any particular mindset or dictated to by dogmas. Consequently, he has really taken to beer. He is extremely enthusiastic about it and always has a lot of inspiring ideas for new ingredients. It was him, for example, who gave me the idea of using the Asian citrus fruit yuzu in one of my beers.

Mielcke also doesn't hesitate to think in reverse about the relationship between beer and food. Because why should food always dictate what beer you drink? As Jakob says, it takes me several months to make a beer, and I can't change it once it's finished, whereas it takes him five seconds to make a change to a dish, for example by making it more or less salty, so that it goes better with the beer. Very few sommeliers would say, 'We'll choose this wine and then the chef will prepare a dish for it'. Even though it's evident that food and wine would go even better together if you did that instead.

In the following pages, you will find a number of tips on how to approach beer – in terms of taste, aroma and feeling, when it comes to matching beer with good food. Furthermore, a number of Mikkeller's friends and partners have contributed dishes created especially for beer. This gives you the opportunity to select the right beer for your meal, but also to turn the relationship between food and beer on its head and prepare and season dishes that some of the world's best chefs have designed specifically for a particular Mikkeller beer.

Before we start, I would like to add, however, that I am by no means of the opinion that beer has to be drunk with refined food. In my view, a pale ale can be just as suitable with street food in Bangkok or open sandwiches in Amager as with a Michelin-starred dish. My mission is simply to open people's eyes to what beer can offer in relation to food – and hopefully help to break down the misconception that gourmet food is inseparably linked with wine.

WHAT BEER SHOULD YOU DRINK WITH YOUR FOOD?

Here are some general guidelines for what types of beer go with what types of food. But experiment for yourself. And if you have dinner guests and are in doubt, try serving both wine and beer with your meal. This could also generate some interesting debate on the subject. Remember that the accompaniments are just as important in relation to the choice of beer as whether you are having fish or meat. And, finally, also remember that if you want to serve beer with several courses, it is important not to begin with the strongest, heaviest beers but to slowly increase the intensity to create cohesion in your meal.

Generally, the same considerations apply as when you are putting together wine and food. It is important to find taste nuances in the beer that can complement the taste nuances in the food, but it is just as important to have an appreciation of the food's richness. For example, the basic taste of most types of cabbage goes well with the subtly herbal, slightly sulphury element of many lagers. But you cannot successfully serve the same lager with a light, stir-fried dish of finely chopped cabbage, ginger and fresh herbs as you can with a classic plate of choucroute from Alsace. Here the richness is completely different and needs to be matched by the beer.

FISH AND SHELLFISH

If you are having shellfish or white fish (cod, sole or haddock, for instance) with mild accompaniments such as potatoes, butter sauce and perhaps slightly sour vegetables, weissbier (white beer) or witbier are a fantastic match. Although in themselves they are not the most exciting beer types, in combination with fish and shellfish they can be better than even the finest Chablis.

Remember that shellfish such as scallops, prawns, langoustines and lobster have a sweetish aroma and taste that should ideally be matched by a hint of sweetness in the beer. Witbier and weissbier are extremely dry in themselves but have lots of sweetness in the aroma and are therefore perfect. Try, for example, Mikkeller's 'Vesterbro Wit' or Andech's classic 'Hefe Weisse Hell' (especially good with scallops).

If you are feeling slightly more adventurous, try combining sweet shellfish – especially roasted or grilled – with a sour beer, perhaps with fruit, in the Belgian mould. Mikkeller's 'Spontan' series, for example, is a natural option, but Rodenbach's 'Grand Cru' and Boon's 'Oude Kriek' are also both brilliant choices.

Common mussels, razor shells and similar shellfish have very little sweetness and are therefore really good with slightly hoppier beers that do not have too much body. 'Pilsner Urquell' or 'Jever Pilsener' from Germany are good examples. The very best match for common mussels, however, especially when served classically steamed in white wine or beer, is lambic. Try, for example, Drie Fonteinen's 'Oude Gueuze', Mikkeller's 'Spontanale' or Girardin's 'Black Label Gueze'.

Oysters are another story altogether because of their strong taste, at least in the case of Danish oysters. The most pervasive component of the taste of oysters is salt. And it is the salt that means that oysters, contrary to popular perception, are actually not a good match for wine. The prominent salty taste clashes with the wine's fruit and sourness and can sometimes make the wine seem slightly metallic in taste. Beer, on the other hand, can counteract the salt through the bitterness from the hops.

When you combine beer and oysters, it is generally sensible to forego fruity beer and instead look for something that primarily offers freshness, dryness and bitterness. Avoid pale ale and IPA, both of which have too much fruitiness, and instead opt for a good lager such as 'Greed' from Amager Bryghus or a Czech 'Staropramen'.

MEAT

With slightly heavier dishes of meat – steak or chicken – accompanied by, for example, grilled vegetables and a rich sauce, hoppy, sweet India pale ales or brown ales with a lot of body are a really good match. Try, for example, Mikkeller's 'Green Gold', 'Jackie Brown' or 'American Dream'. The latter is especially good with chicken with lighter accompaniments such as salad.

Remember that the more fatty the meat, the more bitter the beer should be because taste wise the bitterness helps to cut through the fat. Beef with strong, dark sauces can also be accompanied by stout or porter – the sweeter the sauce, the more sweetness the beer can have. Mikkeller's 'Milk Stout' is a good option here

SPICY/ RICH MEAT

Hoppy beers such as pale ales and India pale ales without too much sweetness go well with spicy dishes, grilled dishes, lamb and game, for example grilled entrecote with herb butter and roast vegetables or slow-cooked pig's cheek with mashed potato and port wine gravy. Choose, for example, To Øl's 'First Frontier' or 'Dangerously Close But No Cigar', Mikkeller's 'Mosaic IIPA' or 'Single Hop Amarillo'. Three Floyds' 'Alpha King' and AleSmith's 'IPA' are also well worth trying.

CHEESE

Sweet beers such as dubbel, quadrupel and Scottish ales go really well with cheese, especially if you also have a little fruit compote or honey. Try, for example, Mikkeller's 'Monks Eliksir' or 'Big Worse'. The big, dark Belgian beers also come into their own here, for example St. Bernardus's 'Abt 12' or 'Westvleteren 12'

DESSERT

Wine has many enemies when it comes to food: eggs, asparagus, herrings (in vinegar) and grapes, for example. The achilles heel of beer is probably dessert. For beer meals, the biggest challenge is always finding a beer that matches the dessert, but there are some good basic rules.

With a light and fresh fruit dessert, such as sorbet, without too much sweetness and with red or black berries, you should choose a lighter beer without too much sweetness and, ideally, with a little fruit. This could be Mikkeller's 'Monks Eliksir' or a sweet lambic such as Timmerman's 'Framboise' or 'Kriek'. Lindeman's 'Apple' is also a good option.

With heavier, sweeter desserts, for example chocolate ice cream or chocolate cake, sweet stouts and porters are generally a good bet. The main rule is that if a sweet dessert wine goes well, so too does a sweet beer. Try, for example, To Øl's 'By Udder Means' (BA Muscatel), or Mikkeller's 'Beer Geek Brunch Weasel' or 'Milk Stout'. American imperial stouts such as AleSmith's 'Speedway Stout' or Cigar City's 'Marshall Zhukov' are also good choices.

Last, but not least, De Dolle Brouwers' 'Stille Nacht', which is not only the world's best dessert beer but possibly one of the world's best beers overall, goes brilliantly with light desserts (without chocolate) incorporating caramel in some form or other, for example crème brûlée, crème caramel or tarte tatin.

FOOD RECIPES

... & FRIENDS

The following five recipes were created by some of the world's most skilful chefs, all of whom are masters of a range of advanced cooking techniques – from the classical and traditional to the modern and molecular. For this reason, most of the dishes are relatively complicated to recreate at home, but if you are adventurous you can easily give them a go. The recipes have been compiled so that you can follow them step by step in your own kitchen. However, it may be advisable to read them through before you start. You will then be prepared for how much time, effort, equipment and technical ability are required.

If you don't have the courage to go all out and make a whole meal, you can easily pick individual components and recycle them in less complicated meals. The recipes offer lots of possibilities for pepping up everyday dishes or putting an ace on your dinner-party menu. Or you could just use them as inspiration: they give a unique insight into the engine room of modern gastronomy and offer a number of very specific examples showing how beer and food can be combined in new, unexpected ways and how a dish can be composed of different tastes and textures to complement the beer – and not vice versa.

NOMA

EFollowing a beer tasting for Noma's staff at Mikkeller
Bar, the restaurant's then sommelier,Pontus Eloffson,
contacted Mikkeller to ask whether we would brew a beer for
Noma. This was the ultimate seal of approval for Mikkeller
in the gourmet world and helped spread our name in
gastronomic circles around the world. At the same time, it
was an interesting challenge to brew for a restaurant such as
Noma. Mikkeller is famous for making extreme beer, but that
sort of beer doesn't fit in well with Noma's delicate Nordic
cuisine. The beer had to match their food, which required a
completely new approach by me – a very different balancing
act. The initial result was Noma Novel – a light, pale and
refreshing Belgian inspired beer with lots of carbonic acid.
Later, I was asked to brew Pontus – a witbier containing
samphire – to mark the occasion of Pontus leaving Noma.

GRILLED FLATBREAD WITH GOTLAND TRUFFLES

SERVED WITH MIKKELLER'S PONTUS

For 4 people

LACTIC CEP WATER

500g (1lb 2oz) frozen cep
  mushrooms
15g (½oz) sea salt (without
  added iodine)

CEP OIL

200g (7oz) grapeseed oil

TRUFFLE PURÉE

2 x 50g 1¾oz) yeast
50g (1¾oz) grapeseed oil
40g (1½oz) frozen Gotland
  truffles

BLACK GARLIC WATER

25g (1oz) black garlic

FLATBREAD

75g (2¾oz) tipo 00 flour
1g (a pinch) malt flour
15g (½oz) sieved koji powder
  (preferably fresh)
40g (1½oz) Mikkeller Pontus
1.5g (a pinch) salt
5g (¼oz) butter (room
  temperature)
10g (¼oz) rose oil

FLOUR MIX

60g (2oz) tipo 00 flour
5g (¼oz) malt flour

WALNUT PASTE

3.5g (⅛oz) black garlic
1g (a pinch) raw garlic
45g (1½oz) blanched, roasted
  walnuts

MISCELLANEOUS

12 boiled spinach leaves
24 truffle slices (depending
  on size)

1. LACTIC CEP WATER

(start 4–5 days in advance)

Place the frozen ceps in a sterilized airtight container (they should not fill more than half of the container).

Add salt and mix in – either with a sterilized spoon or with your fingers wearing a latex glove to avoid infection.

Close the container and store in a dark place at room temperature (e.g. a kitchen cupboard).

The ceps will probably need 2-3 days before they are ready, but check on them once in a while. They are ready when they bubble gently and give off a good mushroom aroma (if you suspect mould in the container, you should discard the ceps and start again).

Place the ceps into a sieve over a bowl.

Cover with cling-film and place the sieve and bowl in the fridge overnight to extract as much liquid as possible from the ceps into the bowl.

Measure out 250g (9fl oz) of liquid and freeze it to ice in the freezer. Save the rest of the liquid in the fridge.

Spread out the surplus cep flesh in a roasting pan containing greaseproof paper.

Heat the ceps in the oven at 60°C (140°F) until they are completely dry. Save the dried ceps for later.

2. LACTIC CEP OIL AND PASTE

(start the day before)

Blend the dried cep flesh into a purée.

Spread the purée out in a thin layer on a piece of greaseproof paper and leave to air-dry overnight. This will give you a lovely, almost completely dry sheet with roughly the consistency of fruit leather (called lactic cep leather).

Blend the grapeseed oil with 100g (3½oz) of cep leather in a Thermomixer for 8 min at high speed. Alternatively, use an ordinary blender, although it will need to be powerful and have a relatively wide bowl.

Place the ceps into a fine sieve and allow the oil (called lactic cep oil) to drip into a bowl.

Return the remaining cep flesh from the sieve to the blender and blend again at high speed into a smooth paste.

Place the paste back in the sieve and allow the oil to drip down.

Save the paste (called lactic cep paste) for later.

3. TRUFFLE PURÉ

(start the day before)

Remove the truffles from the freezer to thaw.

Halve the two 'yeast squares' and place them in the oven at 120°C (245°F) for 30 min.

Leave to cool so they become hard and then blend them with the grapeseed oil for approx. 8 min until the mixture is soft.

Leave to infuse overnight, then pour the mixture into a fine sieve so the oil can drain out into a bowl.

Blend 10g (¼oz) of the oil with the thawed truffles and 5g of cep water to a purée consistency.

Put to one side.

4. BLACK GARLIC WATER

(start in the morning)

Remove the 250g (9oz) of cep ice from the freezer.

You are now ready to carry out ice filtration: Place the ice in a sieve lined with a cloth and let it drip into a bowl as it thaws. This will make the liquid completely clear.

Place the black garlic cloves in cold water to soak for 30 min, then bake in the oven at 60°C (140°F) for 3 hours. Ordinary ovens are not usually particularly good at delivering the precise temperature, so you might want to use a roasting thermometer (placed in the middle of the oven) to get the right heat.

Press the black garlic through a fine sieve and whisk together with the ice-filtered cep water.

Place to one side.

5. FLATBREAD

(on the day)

Mix all the dry ingredients with the beer and the rose oil. Use a dough scraper to prevent the dough becoming overkneaded.

Divide the dough into four portions and pass the portions through a pasta machine on setting 2 (or roll them out using a rolling-pin). At Noma, we normally use 9g (¼oz) for each portion, but if you want larger flatbreads, you can easily use double or treble the amount.

Mix the flour mix together and sprinkle it lightly over the dough.

6. WALNUT PASTE

(on the day)

Use a mortar to mix the ingredients: First crush the garlic, then add the blanched, roasted walnuts.

When the consistency is soft, add 7g (¼oz) of cep paste and then 15g of cep oil.

Finish by seasoning the mixture with salt and pepper. If necessary, adjust the consistency. It should be roughly like a tapenade.

Place to one side.

BEFORE SERVING

Place the four flatbreads on a warm grill or grill pan.

Turn them as soon as they puff up and keep turning them at regular intervals until they are ready. Take care not to burn them.

Leave the flatbreads standing in a dry pan at low temperature so they keep warm. Alternatively, leave them in the oven at 60°C (140°F).

Spread a thin layer of walnut paste onto the flatbreads and spray generously with cep oil using an atomizer. Alternatively, drizzle the oil on, although this does not produce the same result.

Fry the spinach on a piece of lightly oiled greaseproof paper in a pan.

Arrange the spinach on the flatbreads and give them a spray with black garlic water.

Squeeze a little truffle paste onto the flatbreads using an icing bag.

Arrange a suitable number of truffle slices on top of the dish and then spray with a good dose of cep oil.

Sprinkle with coarse salt and serve with Mikkeller's 'Pontus'.

MIELCKE&
HURTIGKARL

In recent years, Jakob Mielcke, chef and owner of Mielcke & Hurtigkarl, has been one of my closest partners when it comes to beer and food. Among other things, we have held beer dinners at his restaurant in conjunction with the American brewery Three Floyds and the Belgian De Struise Brouwers. We have also run beer and food events together in San Francisco and Texas and created the 'Mad Beer' series consisting of five different beers – 'Bitter', 'Salt', 'Sour', 'Sweet' and 'Umami'. The series was brewed with the specific purpose of creating a range of beers that unite beer and food in the best possible way. For Mielcke & Hurtigkarl, Mikkeller has brewed the house beer 'Mielcke & Hurtigkarl' – a Belgian blonde ale aged in wine barrels from the French Château d'Yquem.

CHERRY AND MISO

SERVED WITH MIKKELLER'S 'SPONTAN CHERRY FREDERIKSDAL'

BEETROOT JELLY

500ml (1pt) beetroot juice
50g (1¾oz) sugar
Vanilla seeds from half a pod
6.5g (¼oz) agar

CHERRY COMPOTE

500g (1lb 2oz) oxheart cherries
1 vanilla pod
Peel from 2 lemons
100g (3½oz) dark cane sugar
15 large, red shiso leaves

LAVENDER CREAM

300ml (½ pt) fresh cream
3 whole lavender flowers

BAKED MARZIPAN

100g (3½oz) marzipan

GARNISH

Lavatera trimestris
shiso sprouts

WHITE MISO ICE CREAM

500ml (1pt) milk
250ml (½pt) cream
125g (4½oz) Kyoto miso plus
100g (3½oz) ordinary white miso
100ml (3⅓fl oz) size 0 egg yolks
110g (3¾oz) sugar

1. BEETROOT JELLY

Mix all the ingredients together in a saucepan and add a little lemon juice.

Bring to the boil and allow to boil thoroughly for approx. 2 minutes.

Place in the refrigerator and leave to set.

Blend into a smooth cream.

2. CHERRY COMPOTE

Halve the cherries and remove the stones.

Place all the ingredients, including the stones, in a saucepan.

Cut a piece of greaseproof paper to fit the saucepan and lay it over the cherries.

Leave the cherries to simmer for approx. 3 hours until they have boiled down. The cherries should remain intact, so it is important to keep a close eye on the heat during the processs.

Leave the stones with the fruit to add flavour.

3. LAVENDER CREAM

Gently mix the cream and lavender flowers together using a stick blender without allowing the cream to start thickening.

Leave to stand for 2 hours, then sieve out the flowers.

4. BAKED MARZIPAN

Grate the marzipan using a coarse grater.

Bake at 160°C (320°F) until golden and crisp.

Arrange all the elements as desired and garnish with *Lavatera trimestris* and shiso sprouts.

Serve with Mikkeller's 'Spontan Cherry Frederiksdal'.

5. WHITE MISO ICE CREAM

Place the milk, cream and miso in a small saucepan.

Heat until almost boiling. Meanwhile whisk the eggs and sugar together in a separate bowl until smooth

Pour a little of the hot mixture from the saucepan into the bowl while whisking, then pour all the contents of the bowl into the saucepan

Heat the contents of the saucepan, stirring continuously until they thicken (at approximately 85°C/185°F). Remove from the heat immediately.

Sieve the mixture, then freeze it, ideally in an ice cream maker. Alternatively, place the mixture in the freezer and stir every 30 minutes.

If you want the ice cream to be really fluffy, you can freeze it in a Pacojet beaker.

AMASS

I got to know Amass's chef and main man Matthew Orlando when he was working as a chef at Noma. When he went solo and opened his own restaurant in Refshaleøen, we agreed that Mikkeller would brew a house beer for it. Matthew hails from San Diego, so it was an obvious choice to brew a West Coast-inspired IPA with lots of hops. Given that Amass is located at the former site of the B&W shipyard in Refshaleøen in the Port of Copenhagen, we later made a 'Red' beer, which was inspired by the dark lager that the workers drank during B&W's golden age a hundred years ago.

SALTED LAMB BREAST <u>WITH</u> CARAMEL MALT

SERVED WITH MIKKELLER'S 'BLACK'

500g (1lb 2oz) lamb breast

1 bottle Mikkeller's 'Black'

100g (3½oz) caramel malt (available in any brewing store)

18 small, red beetroots

5 large, red beetroots

25g (1oz) dried ceps

120g (4oz) grapeseed oil

4 large cloves garlic (fermented garlic)

20g (¾oz) freeze-dried blackcurrants

100g (3½oz) sea salt

PREPARATION, STAGE 1

(ideally the day before)

Sprinkle plenty of salt onto the raw lamb breast and place it in a container before covering it with caramel malt.

Leave to infuse in the fridge for 8 hours or overnight

Wipe off the caramel malt using a clean tea towel (it's okay if some malt is left on the lamb).

Place the lamb breast in a vacuum bag together with 100ml (3½ fl oz) of Mikkeller's 'Black'.

Vacuum seal the bag and cook the whole thing with a weight on top in a steam oven at 90°C (194°F) for 1 hour 40 min.

Remove the lamb from the oven and leave to cool fully in the bag.

PREPARATION, STAGE 2

(on the day)

Place two small beetroots to one side for later and pack the rest in tinfoil together with a little salt and 20g (¾oz) of grapeseed oil.

Bake in the oven at 160°C (320°F) until the beetroots are tender.

Squeeze the juice from the large beetroots and place them in a pan together with 10g (¼oz) of dried ceps.

Reduce the liquid by three quarters on the hob until you end up with a beetroot reduction.

PREPARATION, STAGE 3

(on the day)

Pour 100g (3½oz) of grapeseed oil into another pan and add the remaining dried ceps.

Heat the oil to 90°C (194°F) before removing the pan from the heat and leaving the oil to stand and infuse for 1 hour.

Sieve the ceps from the oil.

PREPARATION, STAGE 4

(on the day)

Remove the skin from the small baked beetroots and quarter them.

Take the two remaining beetroots and cut them into thin slices.

Place both lots of beetroot to one side.

SERVERING AND GARNISHING

Divide the lamb breast into four and roast the portions skin-side down for around 2-3 min until the skin is crispy.

Heat the baked beetroot quarters in the beetroot reduction and arrange them on the plate with a spoon.

Cut each clove of garlic into six pieces and arrange them together with the baked beetroots.

Place a piece of roast lamb on the plate and garnish with dried blackcurrants, thin slices of beetroot and a splash of cep oil.

Arrange the remaining portions in the same way. Drink the rest of the oil; you've earned it!

KIIN KIIN

In addition to our collaboration on the 'Wine vs Beer' events, Mikkeller and Henrik Yde-Andersen have produced a number of beers in tandem with all Yde-Andersen's Asian-inspired restaurants. Of all the world's cuisines, Asian is my favourite, so it's been fun to brew a range of beers to accompany Asian food. The beers we have made include a lager with lemon and lime peel for Kiin Kiin and a lager with lemongrass and coriander for the restaurant Dim Sum. In 2013, we also hosted a beer dinner together in Bangkok at Yde-Andersen's Thai answer to Kiin Kiin, Sra Bua.

AUBERGINE RELISH <u>WITH</u> S<u>M</u>OKED MARROWBONE <u>AND</u> PORK CRACKLING

SERVERES WITH MIKKELLER'S 'DIM SUM'

300g (10½oz) aubergine

100g (3½oz) large green chilis

100g (3½oz) onion

20g (¾oz) garlic

15g (½oz) small green chilis

2kg (4½lbs) marrowbone

1kg (2¼lbs) pork skin

1 handful shiso

vinegar

fish sauce

salt

PREPARING THE MARROW

(start 3 days beforehand)

Remove the marrow from the bones and place it in a 10% brine for three days.

The marrow now needs to be cold-smoked. You can buy a small smoking machine quite cheaply, but there is lots of information on the web on how best to carry out smoking.

Cut the marrow into slices and fry it in a little oil in a pan.

PREPARING THE PIG SKIN

(ideally start the day before)

Boil the pig skin in water with a little vinegar.

When the skin is tender, it needs to dry (this can be done in an oven at 45°C (113°F).

Scrape any fat from the skin and fry the skin in very hot oil until it has puffed up.

BEFORE SERVING

Halve the aubergines and grill them thoroughly on the skin side.

Also thoroughly grill the large and small green chilis.

Remove the flesh from both the aubergines and the chilis and chop them coarsely before stirring them into a paste.

Add finely chopped onion and garlic and give the paste a quick boil.

Season with fish sauce and salt, then arrange in a halved marrowbone with crispy crackling and marrow pieces.

Garnish with shiso and serve with Mikkeller's 'Dim Sum'.

MISSION CHINESE

In connection with Mikkeller's bar opening in San Francisco, I visited the city on a number of occasions. Each time, I ate out at the restaurant Mission Chinese because I love their fresh approach to Chinese cuisine and because I really like the special laid-back set-up and atmosphere at the restaurant, which is rather unique. Many times I ended up sitting and drinking beer with the staff after closing time, and that resulted in a collaboration, 'Mission Chinese', a smoked lager with sichuan pepper.

Foto: Alanna Hale

CHONGQING CHICKEN WINGS

SERVED WITH MIKKELLER'S 'MISSION CHINESE'

For 4 people

500g (1lb 2oz) chicken wings
(preferably the middle section of the wing)
3 tbsp salt
4 litres (8½ pts) oil (for frying)

SPICE MIX
1 tbsp salt
1 tbsp sugar
1 tbsp cayenne powder
2 tbsp fennel seeds
1 tsp sichuan peppercorns
½ tsp star anise
½ tsp cardamom
½ tsp caraway
½ tsp cloves
500g (1lb 2oz) tianjin chili

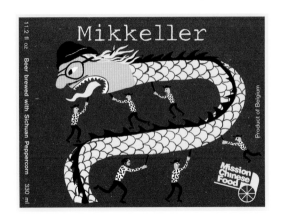

PREPARATION

(start 2 days beforehand)

Salt the wings thoroughly in a bowl with approx. 3 tbsp salt and put them in the freezer overnight.

Heat the oil to 160°C (320°F) and fry the wings for 6-7 mins. If necessary, fry in batches

Remove the wings and leave them to cool.

Put the wings in the freezer overnight uncovered. The freezing will cause the moisture in the skin to crystallize and crack, which will make the wings extra crispy when they are re-fried.

COOKING

(on the day)

Turn on the oven at 180°C (356°F).

Heat the oil to 180°C (356°F) in a large pan or a fryer.

Roast the spices and grind them up.

Fry the wings in the hot oil for 4-6 minutes until they are golden and slightly crispy. At the same time, bake the tianjin chilis at 180°C (356°F) in the oven.

Place the wings in a bowl together with the baked chilis and fold them all together. The aim is to create an aromatic accompaniment that perfumes the dish.

Put the wings in a bowl and drizzle on the spice mix. The wings will crisp up as they cool down.

Place all the wings and the aromatic chilis on a plate and serve with a cold Mikkeller 'Mission Chinese'.

BEER RETAILERS

GOOD STORES

MIKKELLER & FRIENDS BOTTLE SHOP
Copenhagen, Denmark

ØLBUTIKKEN
Copenhagen, Denmark

BEERS OF EUROPE
www.beersofeurope.co.uk

THE BEER BOUTIQUE
134 Upper Richmond Road, London SW15 2SP

BOTTLE DOG
69 Grays Inn Rd, London, WC1X 8TR

UTOBEER
Borough Market, London SE1 1TL

ARTISAN BEER DEPOT
2482 W. El Camino Real,
Mountain View, CA 94040, USA

CRAFT SHACK
www.craftshack.com

PORT CHESTER BEER STORE
315 North Main Street, Port Chester,
NY 10573, USA

THE WINE CLUB
953 Harrison Street, San Francisco, CA94107, USA

WEST LAKEVIEW LIQUORS
Chicago, Illinois
www.wlvliquors.com

SELECTED BEER BARS

EUROPE

SCANDINAVIA

MIKKELLER BAR
Copenhagen, Denmark

MIKKELLER & FRIENDS
Copenhagen, Denmark

MIKROPOLIS
Copenhagen, Denmark

WAR PIGS
Copenhagen, Denmark

MIKKELLER BAR
Stockholm, Sweden

PUBOLOGI
Stockholm, Sweden

BISHOP ARMS
Stockholm, Sweden

CARDINAL
Stavanger, Norway

BELGIUM

CHEZ MOEDER LAMBIC
Brussels, Belgium

BIER CIRCUS
Brussels, Belgium

DE DOLLE BROUWERS
Esen, Belgium

KULMINATOR
Antwerp, Belgium

**DE HEEREN
VAN LIEDERKERCKE**
Denderleeuw, Belgium

NETHERLANDS

BEER TEMPLE
Amsterdam, Netherlands

GOLLEM
Amsterdam, Netherlands

UK

**KING WILLIAM
THE FOURTH**
London, England

BREWDOG BARS
London, England

KERNEL BREWERY
London, England

DUKE'S BREW & QUE
London, England

USA

MIKKELLER BAR
San Francisco, CA

THE TRAPPIST
Oakland, CA

NORTHDOWN
Chicago, Ill

LOCAL OPTION
Chicago, Ill

THE MAP ROOM
Chicago, Ill

**THREE FLOYDS
BREWING CO. & BREWPUB**
Munster, USA

TØRST
New York, NY

SPUYTEN DUYVIL
New York, NY

THE BIG HUNT
Washington, USA

ARMSBY ABBEY
Massachusetts, USA

PIZZAPORT BREWPUB
Carlsbad, CA

ASIA

MIKKELLER
Bangkok, Thailand

CRAFT HEAD
Tokyo, Japan

BAKUSHU CLUB POPEYE
Tokyo, Japan

BOXING CAT BREWPUB
Shanghai, China

TAPS BEER BAR
Kuala Lumpur, Malaysia

SOURCES

THE FOLLOWING SOURCES HAVE BEEN USED IN THE MAKING OF THIS BOOK.

BOOKS

CARSTEN BERTHELSEN
Øl for enhver smag (2008)

CARSTEN BERTHELSEN AND CARSTEN KYSTER
Godt bryg, god mad (2012)

GARRETT OLIVER (Ed)
The Oxford Companion to Beer (2011)

RUNA FLÜGGE, CAMILLA HÜNICHE,
STEFAN BRIX AND KRISTIAN JENSEN
Danske mikrobryggerier – succes, fiasko, fremtid (2013)

THOMAS HORNE AND COLIN EICK
Beer Brewing– Fra hånd til munn (2013)

TOM ACITELLI
*The Audacity of Hops
– The History of America's Craft Beer Revolution (2013)*

ARTICLES

Længe leve revolutionen
BY MARCUS AGGERSBJERG, *Gastro*

FILMS

BRITISH LOCAL HISTORIES SERIES:
The History of CAMRA (The Campaign for Real Ale) (2011)

OTHER

BREWERS ASSOCIATION
Beer Style Guidelines (2011)

INTERVIEWS

MIKKEL BORG BJERGSØ

TOBIAS EMIL JENSEN

CARSTEN BERTHELSEN

SØREN HOUMØLLER

THOMAS HOELGAARD

FREDRIK JOHANSEN

THOMAS SCHØN

KRISTIAN KELLER

DIRK NAUDTS

INTERNET

www.ale.dk

www.beeradvocate.com

www.beerticker.dk

www.brewersassociation.org

www.camra.org.uk

www.denstoredanske.dk

www.haandbryg.dk

www.historienet.dk

www.hopunion.com

www.ratebeer.com

www.sierranevada.com

INDEX

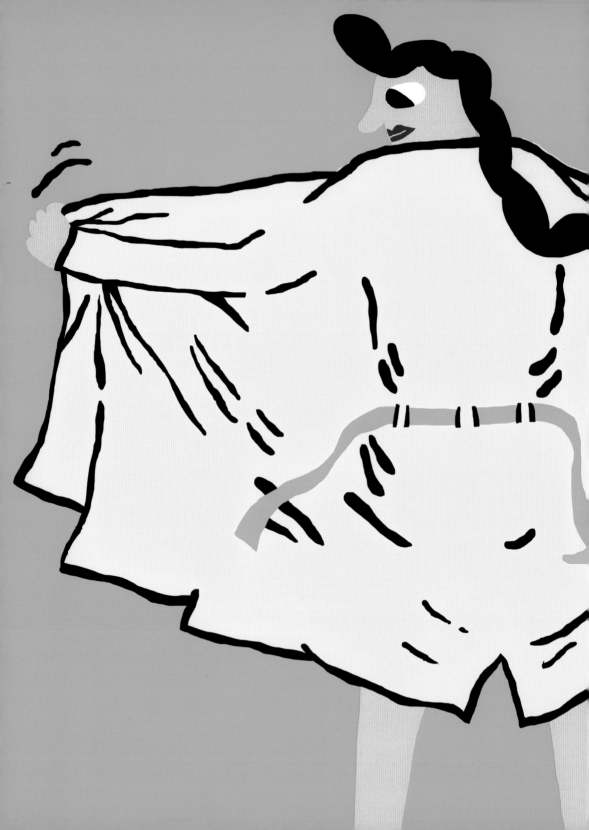

MANY THANKS TO ...

CAMILLA STEPHAN

CARSTEN BERTHELSEN

FREDRIK JOHANSEN

JACOB ALSING

JAKOB MIELCKE

KEITH SHORE

PÄR SJÖLINDER

LASSE EMIL MØLLER

MALTBAZAREN

NILO ZAND

RASMUS MALMSTRØM

THOMAS HOELGAARD

THOMAS SCHØN

TOBIAS EMIL JENSEN

TORE GYNTHER

... & MIKKELLER FRIENDS

MIKKELLER'S BOOK OF BEER

First published in Danish in 2014 by Gyldendal A/S, Denmark

This English language edition first published in 2015 by

Jacqui Small LLP
74-77 White Lion Street
London N1 9PF

ISBN: 978 1 909342 88 0

A catalogue record for this book is available from the British Library.

2017 2016 2015

10 9 8 7 6 5 4 3 2 1

Design: Maria Bramsen
Illustrator: Keith Shore
Photography: Rasmus Malmstrøm and Camilla Stephan
Editor: Troels Hven
Translator: Ray Ashman

This book is typeset in Avenir, Latin Modern and Typewriter.

Printed in Latvia

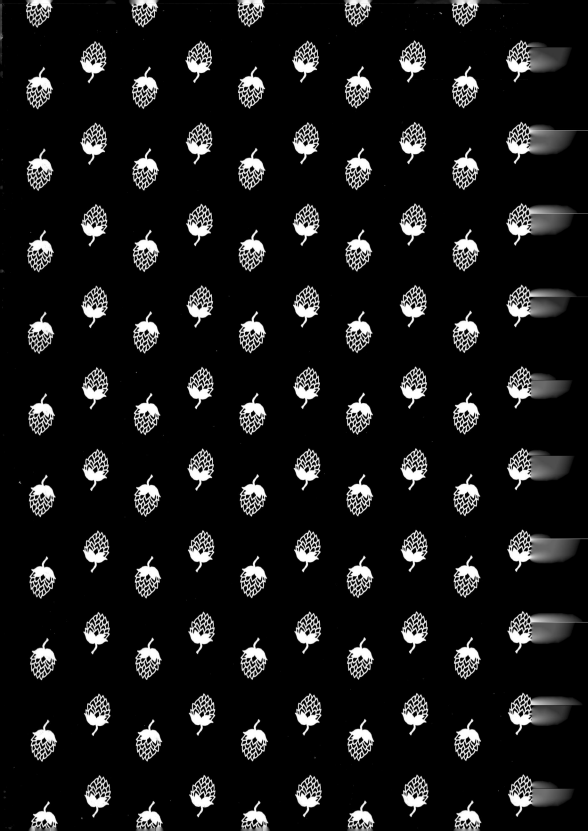